FOREX TRADING FOR BEGINNERS:

SIMPLE STRATEGIES TO LEARN BASICS SYSTEMS TO FIND THE WAY TO INVESTING IN CRYPTOCURRENCY GET YOUR FINANCIAL FREEDOM CATCHING THE RIGHT NEWS USING METHODS AND ANALYSIS.

© **Copyright 2019 - All rights reserved.**

The content contained within this book may not be reproduced, duplicated or transmitted without direct written permission from the author or the publisher.

Under no circumstances will any blame or legal responsibility be held against the publisher, or author, for any damages, reparation, or monetary loss due to the information contained within this book. Either directly or indirectly.

Legal Notice:

This book is copyright protected. This book is only for personal use. You cannot amend, distribute, sell, use, quote or paraphrase any part, or the content within this book, without the consent of the author or publisher.

Disclaimer Notice:

Please note the information contained within this document is for educational and entertainment purposes only. All effort has been executed to present accurate, up to date, and reliable, complete information. No warranties of any kind are declared or implied. Readers acknowledge that the author is not engaging in the rendering of legal, financial, medical or professional advice. The content within this book has been derived from various sources. Please consult a licensed professional before attempting any techniques outlined in this book.

By reading this document, the reader agrees that under no circumstances is the author responsible for any losses, direct or indirect, which are incurred as a result of the use of the information contained within this document, including, but not limited to, — errors, omissions, or inaccuracies.

Table of Contents

Introduction

Chapter 1 What Is Forex Trading?

Chapter 2 Forex Terminology

Chapter 3 Forex Markets

Chapter 4 What a Beginner Needs to Know About Forex Trading

Chapter 5 Currency Pairs

Chapter 6 Trading strategies

Chapter 7 More Strategies

Chapter 8 Basics of Technical Analysis

Chapter 9 How to Place Stop Loss

Chapter 10 How to Read Trading Charts

Chapter 11 Currency Futures And Cryptocurrencies

Chapter 12 Developing Your Trading Plan

Conclusion

Introduction

Most novice investors and traders have quite confused ideas when approaching the forex market – trading currencies (or options, or ETFs), or trading in general.

One of the pivotal points that create confusion in the mind of those interested in making their money work for them is the lack of understanding of the crucial difference that exists between trading and investing.

The confusion derives from the fact that in the eyes of the investor or the uneducated and non-conscious trader, they all think that trading and investing are the same thing.

In reality, although they are united by the desire to make a profit, the two operations arise from different logics and follow different rules.

In fact, those who invest in a measure of the value of what they buy (a house, a business, an object of art, etc.), try to buy it at a discounted or otherwise balanced price, and the entire operation is based on the prediction or hope that, over time, the item purchased will increase in value and that this increase in value will automatically be reflected in a corresponding increase in its market price allowing it to be sold for a profit. An easily understandable example of investment is that those who buy agricultural land in the expectation that it will then be buildable.

The greatest investors of history, such as the legendary Warren Buffett, are in fact masters in buying "depreciated quality". Of course, their time horizon is never very short and the value of what they have purchased can remain or even go down for a certain period of time but all these will not cause them to worry excessively.

To be honest, a hardcore, pure forex trader does not care highly about the objective quality or the nature of what he buys, he is only interested in acquiring it at a right price that (in a rather short time frame) he plans to grow, regardless of the fact that the value of what he purchased remains perfectly identical.

In fact, what makes trading possible is simply the fact that the prices of things (and therefore also financial instruments such as shares, bonds, real estate, etc.) may vary regardless of their value. Remember, for every financial product that is trading publicly – the price will fluctuate, with or without reasons.

On an exchange, for an investor, it is crucial to understand what he is buying and what the current and future value of the company he is planning to buy shares is. In other words, investors search quality financial products that are currently depreciated.

On the other hand, for a forex trader, it is sufficient to use tools (generally the graphs evaluated through technical analysis) that allow him to make a forecast of the future price of a currency pair regardless of the actual value of the currency.

To start trading you must meet the following requirements:

- a PC with a stable internet connection;
- an online trading platform;
- all the recommended brokers offer an adequate training to all traders whether they are novice traders or experts;
- graphs relating to market quotes in real time;
- economic news;
- comments and operational suggestions;
- a great desire to learn.

When investing in the forex market, you can do mainly two different types of transactions:

- long (upward speculation)
- short (downward speculation)

In other words, when you are trading, you can buy currencies and sell currencies. The goal, however, remains the same: to make a profit. When you want to buy, you will only get a profit if the value of the currency increased when we want to sell it. For example, we buy 100 lots of a currency when it is worth 1.1$ each, and then we sell them when they're worth 1.2$ each. The price difference equals to our profit.

When you want to sell, it becomes a bit more complicated. In short transactions, in fact, it is the broker that lends us the number of shares on which we want to invest on the downside. For example, the broker can lend us 1,000 euros listed at 1.23$ each. The securities that the broker lends us for a short transaction are sold immediately: the profit remains "frozen" in their trading account.

This profit will be used to buy back the same amount of currency that the broker had lent us because we have to return this currency to the broker. In that case, we will have gains if the value of the currency has fallen.

The difference between the initial sale of the securities lent and the expense to repurchase them is + € 500 in this case. That is our profit. If, on the other hand, the value of the currency increases, we will have to spend more money than those earned from the initial sale of the prearranged securities: in this case, we will suffer a loss.

The main method for investing in the forex market, therefore, remains the classic forex market. When you operate on the forex market, you are actually buying and selling currencies.

However, over the years, other financial instruments have been introduced to invest in forex and currencies indices on the forex exchange. We are talking about CFD (Contract for Difference) and binary options. The main feature of these two financial instruments is the following: when you use them to trade in forex, you will not actually own the currency you are buying, instead you are just betting on the price movement.

That said, for those who do not intend to trade online, it could make little sense. Let's try to clarify. Both CFDs and binary options are contracts between traders and brokers. It's not like the classic forex market, where traders buy and sell among themselves. In CFDs and binary options, the actual asset movement (in this case the buying and selling of currencies) does not take place.

CFDs and binary options are used to speculate on the performance of the value of equity securities. If the trader's forecast is correct, the transaction will lead to a profit; vice versa, if the trader's prediction is wrong, the transaction will lead to a loss. So, the mode of operation is similar to the stock market: if I invest on the upside, whether I do it with CFDs or actually buy currencies, I only earn money if the value increases.

As we explained in the previous paragraphs, CFDs are also derivative instruments, so they are used to speculate on the performance of asset values. This means that when you buy and sell CFDs you will never own the asset traded (as opposed to classic forex trading).

Moreover, as with binary options, with CFDs it is possible to trade on:

    1. Equity securities

2. Equity indices

3. Forex currencies pairs

4. Commodities

5. ETF

Just to give an example, if you use a lever of 1: 100 and invest € 100, thanks to this lever you can move well € 10,000 (using only your hundred!). All this is made possible thanks to the leverage, which is a sort of "loan" (if we can define it) by the broker, thanks to which you can invest more money than you really have.

This means that your earnings, but also your losses, will be calculated not on the € 100 you really invested, but on the € 10,000, you will have invested thanks to leverage. Therefore the lever can, on the one hand, amplify the gains, but also the losses. To see an example of CFD trading, we refer you to our article on how to trade CFDs in equities with eToro. eToro is one of the leading CFD brokers, very suitable also for non-professional traders and those who want to approach the world of online trading (thanks to the free and unlimited demo account offer).

But if we talk about eToro, we cannot talk about Social Trading. For those who do not know, eToro was the first broker to have introduced Social Trading in CFDs. Thanks to Social trading it is possible to invest by copying (automatically) the operations carried out by the other traders registered on the eToro platform. All you need is a couple of clicks to find the traders to follow, choose the amount to invest, and you're done. In this way, even novice traders can exploit the knowledge and experience of professional traders, copying their operations.

The online trading strategies are based on the study of mathematical and graphic analysis that can suggest the trader the best moment to buy and sell. As we have seen today, it is possible to invest in the stock market thanks to online trading, choosing between trading binary options and trading with the forex market.

Precise right away that there is no suitable trading strategy for all traders, but there are different trading strategies, based on traders and their style of trading. Therefore, it is possible to customize different online trading strategies on the basis of their trading objectives, their intellectual and psychological abilities.

We also recommend using 2 proven techniques to not turn winnings into losses:

Stop loss: it establishes a maximum loss that you are willing to suffer;

Take profit: you place a dynamic exit level that rises slowly.

Chapter 1 What Is Forex Trading?

Forex is short for *foreign exchange* and is basically an exchange of currencies. For example, when you are traveling from one country to another, you will need to exchange your home currency for the other country's currency. If you live in the United States and are traveling to Europe, you will need to exchange the American dollar for euros.

Forex is one of the biggest trading markets. One reason is that every country has a currency. The other reason is that most people understand foreign exchange and how it works. Furthermore, everyone participates in forex in some way, whether this is at an individual or business level. The market is open 24 hours a day from Monday morning to Friday evening.

What do we trade in the Forex Market?

The answer is simple – MONEY. Yes, the forex market is all about money in different currencies. For beginners' trading in forex can be confusing because one is not buying anything physical, which is why many tend to be skeptic about forex trading. Well, this book will clarify such ideology. You can consider buying forex as when you buy a share in a country. It is similar to buying a company's stock in the market. The rate of a particular currency represents a direct reflection of the thinking of the market about its present and future health of the currencies economy.

Remember, the Japanese yen example I made at the beginning. Let us assume you decide to buy the yen, what it means is that you are investing in the Japanese economy by buying a share of the country. In order words, you are "banking" on the Japanese economy that it will do well. You are buying this yen with the intention of selling it in the market in order to gain profit.

Generally, the exchange rate of a particular currency against other currencies represents the economic conditions of the economy.

Principles of Forex Trading

Learn the Market's Trends

It is essential for one to be able to predict the changing nature of the foreign exchange market in order to be successful in Forex Trading.

Accordingly, a person should understand the general direction of the marketplace. Trends can be uptrend, downtrend, or sideways trend. Identifying a pattern can profit a person in that he or she will be able to trade with the trend.

Uptrends are trends that move upwards, indicating an appreciation in currency value. Downtrends move downwards as an indication of depreciation in currency value. Sideways trends show that the currencies are neither appreciating nor depreciating.

Stay Focused and Control Your Emotions

Forex Trading is a challenging marketplace that can cause a person to lose confidence and to give up in the toughest of times. That is understandable given that traders put in their hard-earned money.

As a result, when a person experiences loss, he or she can lose focus when negative emotions become overwhelming. Some of the negative emotions a person may experience include panic, frustration, depression, and desperation.

It is, therefore, essential for one to become aware of the negative emotions that result from Forex Trading so that he or she may minimize the emotional effects of loss and remain focused.

Learn Risk Mitigation Tactics

In order to achieve the profits that a person anticipates, the person needs to minimize the likelihood of financial loss.

Since the forex market keeps on changing, the risks, therefore, keep on changing. The most crucial risk management rule is that a person should not risk more than he or she can afford to lose. Traders who are willing to invest more than they make, become very susceptible to Forex Trading risks.

Consequently, a person can mitigate potential losses by placing stop-loss orders, exchanging more than one currency pair, using software programs for help, and limiting the use of financial leverage.

Establish Personal Forex Trading Limits

A person should know when to stop Forex Trading. One can stop Forex Trading when he or she has an unproductive trading plan, or when he or she is continually experiencing losses.

An ineffective Forex Trading plan may not bring trade to an end, but it will not function as well as a trader may expect. In that case, the trader can consider stopping the trade, constantly changing markets, and the decreasing volatility within a particular foreign trading tool may also cause a trader to take a break from Forex Trading.

In addition, when a person is not in a good physical or emotional state, he or she may want to think about taking a break to deal with personal issues.

Use Technology to Your Benefit

Being up-to-date with existing technological developments can be gratifying in Forex Trading.

Given that forex markets utilize the online forum, high-speed internet connections can increase Forex Trading performance significantly. In order to make the most of Forex Trading, a person must take it as a full-time occupation, and he or she must embrace new technologies. Similarly, receiving forex market current information with smartphones makes it possible for forex traders to track trades anywhere.

Forex Trading is an aggressive enterprise that needs a trader to have an equally competitive edge. Therefore, a forex trader needs to maximize his or her business's potential by taking full advantage of the available technology.

Make Use of a Forex Trading Plan

A Forex Trading plan comprises of rules and guidelines that stipulate a forex trader's entry, exit, and money management principles.

A trading plan provides the opportunity for a forex trader to try out a Forex Trading idea before the trader risks real money. In so doing, a trader can access historical information that helps to know whether a Forex Trading plan is feasible and what outcomes he or she can expect.

When a forex trader comes up with a Forex Trading plan that shows potentially favorable outcomes, he or she can use the trading plan in real Forex Trading situations. The idea is for the forex trader to adhere to the trading plan.

Buying or selling currencies outside of the Forex Trading plans, even if a trader makes a profit, is poor trading, which can end any expectation the plan may have had.

Forex Trading Basics

While the concept of forex trading is easy, executing your trades in the market is difficult. This doesn't mean you won't become successful. What it means is that you will need to educate yourself and work hard. The first step anyone should take is to learn as much as possible about forex trading.

Understanding Pairs

The main difference between the stock market and the forex market is that, in forex, you are essentially trading pairs of currency (that is you buy one currency and sell another), while in the stock market, you buy shares of a company. This is not an option when you are forex trading. Whether you are trading, selling, or buying, you have to use pairs. For example, the Japanese yen is often paired against the Canadian dollar and the Euro against the American dollar.

What's a Pip?

A pip is a 1% movement in the currency value. A pip is a basic unit that is used when talking about currency quotes. It is the last number of the quote, so when you are following the movement of two currencies, you observe from the last two digits so that you can say that a currency moved by the number of pips that differentiates the second from the starting figure. The value of the pip is determined from the size of the trade. You make a decision to buy or sell a currency pair depending on your estimation, which is when you make the market order.

Entry Order

When you use an entry order, you enter your currency pair trade at a specific price. If the price of the currency never reaches the specific price, then your trade is not enforced. If the price is reached, then your trade is completed regardless of your presence at the time.

Stop-Loss Order

A stop-loss order is the price at which you want your dealer to exit the trade when the trade moves against your interests. A stop-loss order prevents losses.

1. *Limit*

A limit is the price at which you want the dealer to exit the trade when it's moving in your favor. Knowing when to exit the trade even when things are looking up is useful because you can hardly predict when a currency will start to drop.

2. *Margin*

When you are buying or selling at a good margin, that means that you control a large amount of currency for an initial investment that is way smaller in comparison. For example, a 100-by-1 margin means that you invest $1,000 for a trade of $100,000. Buying and selling on a margin is safe and appealing because the only amount you risk to lose is the amount you invested, but you have the opportunity to profit a greater amount.

Leveraging Ratios

You are betting at leveraging ratios. A $1,000 bet on 1,000 value of the currency is considered 1:1 leverage.

Trading platforms allow you to follow and market currency in a way that creates a profit. When you're successful in trading one currency so that its value increases against the currency you used to buy it, you can make a profit. You are speculating whether the currency will rise or drop. Your chances of profiting essentially increase with the success of your predictions.

With forex, you trade using leverage, which means that you only need to invest a portion of your positions. By using stop-losses, you can prevent losing your investment.

When it comes to currency rates, many factors have an influence. Interest rates, unemployment numbers, political events, and many more affect the country's currency value.

Currencies may rise and fall in different values for different reasons, one of them being large companies exchanging currencies for the purpose of international trading. The time and circulation of market information is also a significant factor. False and accurate information circulating the market can influence banks to swiftly market currencies, which additionally affects the changes in currency values.

3. *Diversification*

You want to ensure you have diversity within your portfolio to tackle risk. In fact, because the forex market is open 24 hours a day during the weekdays, the market holds more diversity. Therefore, don't just focus on the popular currencies, such as the American dollar and Canadian dollar. You may also trade other pairs such as American dollar/British pound (USD/GBP) or American dollar/Japanese Yen (USD/JPY).

What Are the Risks?

While there are many people trading in forex, there are also those who are facing major financial losses. Since forex trading is essentially all about predictions, one of the biggest risks, obviously, is making a wrong prediction. The following are the many risks of forex trading.

The Wrong Mindset

When it comes to any market, you always need to have the right mindset. Take a moment to think about how certain emotions, such as fear or worry, can control your thoughts. You have to find a way to keep your emotions out of the market. Experienced traders call the right mindset the winning mindset. The following are some key characteristics that will help you gain your winning attitude.

1. **You need to be self-disciplined.** You want to make sure that you take all the steps to ensure you are doing what you need to do to reach success. This means that you complete daily research to see how the forex market is doing, and you document all your currencies, trades, and any other information. Fortunately, most marketing platforms keep your information in its history. However, it is always best that you find a way to keep the files on your computer so that you always have them. You follow any rules and

guidelines that your mentor or yourself have set up.

2. **You are also able to keep your emotions in check.** This might mean that you follow certain strategies you set up for yourself, such as deep-breathing exercises. You don't allow yourself to give in to your excitement if a trade goes well or when you see your account balance. While you might smile and be proud of yourself, you don't allow the feeling to take over as you can become too confident. This can lead you to make mistakes, which can put you and your finances in jeopardy.

3. **You understand that mistakes are going to be made.** Instead of focusing on your mistakes and allowing them to control your future decisions, you learn from them. Many traders write down their mistakes in their trading journal or daily reports.

4. **You understand that the market is fluid and are able to adjust to the changes.** For instance, if a price notes that you need to make a change in your portfolio, then you

make a change. Your portfolio is the place where you keep all the currencies that you can sell or trade.

5. **You understand your risk tolerance.** No matter what strategies you use to try to limit your risk, there is always a risk. If you aren't comfortable with a lot of risks, you will want to focus more on trades that are low risk.

Currency-Value Fluctuations

There are internal-market reasons and external reasons for a currency's value changes. Internally, one country's currency can increase while another currency you hold decreases. These fluctuations are often dependent on how many people are buying and selling the currency. For example, if the yen isn't strong, then more people will purchase the yen, which makes the value increase. This could show a decrease in the American dollar in comparison to the yen because traders are using the American dollar to purchase yen. In other words, the more people purchase currency, the stronger its value. The more people sell a currency, the lower its value.

External factors can be anything from politics to other events going on within the country. These are factors that traders cannot control but you should always be aware of. Because of this, many traders will spend at least half an hour every morning going through the news in order to get an idea of what the market is going to look like that day. Doing this will allow you to know if you should purchase a currency or trade one within your portfolio.

Pair	%	Rate	Time		
GBP/USD	82%	1.54260	14:15	▼	04:23
EUR/JPY	82%	135.365	14:15	▼	04:23
GBP/JPY	81%	183.543	14:15	▼	04:23
USD/JPY	73%	118.983	14:15	▼	04:23
USD/CAD	79%	1.25174	14:15	▼	04:23
USD/CHF	73%	0.94890	14:15	▼	04:23
EUR/GBP	78%	0.73751	14:15	▼	04:23
AUD/USD	79%	0.77801	14:15	▼	04:23
AUD/NZD	73%	1.03561	14:15	▼	04:23
NZD/USD	73%	0.75125	14:15	▼	04:23

Broker Risk

While not every trader has a broker, it is important for a beginner to look into a broker. This person can help you learn about the market and give you advice on what moves to take. However, there are broker risks. In order to limit these risks, you want to ensure you can trust your broker. Do some research before you decide to take on a broker. The best way you can do this is by choosing a broker who is part of a government body as it is regulated. Government bodies have to follow guidelines and ethics.

How to Start

Whenever you start trading, you want to ensure you follow certain steps for success.

First, you always want to do your research. You want to learn as much as possible. This means you will read books, join forex trading forums, find a trusted broker, and anything else you feel is necessary. Once you feel like you know forex trading like the back of your hand, you will be able to move on.

Second, ensure you understand the language. Forex trading has its own language. Take your time to learn these terms, and if you have questions, find another trader to discuss your concerns with.

Third, you want to find your trusted broker. This person will help you make decisions and explain the world of investing to you. Take your time to find the best broker for you. Your broker will help you set up an account.

Fourth, take time to analyze the forex market. Learn about the charts and what they mean. Look back in the history of some currencies so you can gain a better understanding of trading. For example, charts can help you analyze the best time for trading and which currencies are best within the market and help you find the best currencies.

Fifth, if you are trading full-time, set up an office and your schedule. You want to find time to ensure you are self-disciplined enough that you won't struggle with distractions. Take the time to set a start date.

Sixth, once your day arrives, start trading. Make sure that you go through your morning routine, such as reading the paper and seeing how the currencies are doing. Notice any changes that occurred overnight. You also want to ensure you go through your daily schedule and close out your day with your evening routine. For example, check your stocks for the day, and discuss anything about your day in your journal.

How to Profit

Once you start trading, you will want to do what you can to limit your risks. While you will always have some risk, you can find a comfortable level of risk. Another way to profit is by diversifying your portfolio. This means that you will have different currencies and not focus on the same ones.

You also want to be patient. Forex trading is not a get-rich-quick scheme. It will take time to start seeing a profit. Don't give up, and don't fall into the wrong mindset. If you need any help, talk to your broker, a mentor, or someone in the forum. There are many experienced forex traders who are happy to help beginners.

Continue to communicate with your broker, mentor, and anyone on the forum. Even if you spend months researching, people will always be important when it comes to your success. Don't allow yourself to get into the mindset that you know everything. Continue to learn as much as possible. Take time to practice analyzing reports. You have to do whatever you need to so you feel comfortable as a trader.

Types of Trading and Traders

Scalping

There are four main different types of trading within forex trading namely; position trading, swing trading, scalping and day trading. On scalping as a type of trading, very little amount of time is spent on trading. This mostly occurs when the forex market is at its busiest state. Traders who trade in such a way are always looking to trade for just a few minutes while they open many trades in a short period of time. They get small pips as possible and they aim to make a profit from the small pips and many trades opened. It is a strategy to benefit from when the forex market is in full force.

Forex scalpers are dealers who buy or sell currencies, hold on to the exchanged currencies, and then wait for them to have higher and favorable exchange rates before the dealers can change their new currencies back to their original versions.

The scalpers hold deals for seconds to minutes and open and close several positions within a single day. In other words, scalpers go in and out of positions several times each day.

Scalpers trade currencies based on real-time analysis. Scalpers aim to make a profit by selling or buying currencies and holding on to them for a short time before buying or selling the currencies back to the forex market for small gains.

Therefore, that means that scalpers should love sitting in front of their laptops or computers for the entire forex session without taking their eyes off the screen.

Scalping is widespread moments after essential data releases and interest rate announcements. That is because high-impact reports generate significant price moves within a short period.

However, while profits can accrue rapidly with profitable trades, huge losses can also accumulate if the scalper is using a faulty system or if the trader does not understand what he or she is doing.

Swing Trading

Swing trading, unlike scalping in forex exchange, involves the traders opening trades that last for a few days before closing them. The type of traders in this category often analyze the graphs and charts for just a few hours throughout the days, and as the name suggests, they only swing by at certain limited hours of the day. They make decisions based on their evaluations from this single specific time, and will only be back to forex trading at the same time the following day or when they receive notifications from their different platforms of actions needed to be taken. A few days will do for their trades to last.

Swing traders take hold of a position over a few days to several weeks. They hold places for more than one trading session, although not longer than several weeks or a couple of months.

Swing traders aim to capture huge potential price moves. Some swing traders may look for volatile stocks with constant movements, whereas others prefer stock prices that are more predictable.

Swing traders have exposure to overnight and weekend risks, where prices could rift and open the following forex session with markedly different rates. However, swing traders can generate profit by using established risk or reward strategies that will help them to determine where they will enter assets, where they will place stop-loss orders, and to know where they can make profits. Stop-loss orders help to limit the loss when stock prices fall.

Swing traders come up with plans and strategies that will give them an advantage over may trades. The traders do that by looking for trade arrangements that facilitate predictable price movements in the price of the asset. However, no trade arrangement works every time.

Day Trading

This type of trading is usually on a day to day basis. Traders in this category open a trade at the start of the trading period and close off the same trade at the close of the day. When opening a trade at the beginning of the day, these traders often make decisions based on their predictions on how the day in the forex market is going to turn out. The outcome is unpredicted and may turn out to be a loss or a profit at the end of the day.

Forex day traders control trading positions during each trading day. Day traders close the trading positions at the end of the trading day and ensure that there are no positions that remain open during the night.

Forex day traders use currency day trading systems that regulate whether to buy or sell a currency pair in the foreign exchange market. A currency pair is the quotation of two different currencies where the trader quotes the value of one currency in comparison to the other.

Day traders target day currencies that are very liquid to leverage their capital as soon as investment prices change in favorable directions. The traders pick a price position at the start of the day, act on their assessments, and finish the trading day with either a profit or a loss.

Forex day traders avoid holding positions overnight because that may result in stock price gaps, a consequence, which can be very costly.

Position Trading

This is a long term type of trading that ranges from opening trades that go on for a few days and may go up to several years. Traders who are position traders analyzes their trades using the fundamental matters global wise, where their decisions on opening and closing trades are based on this.

Position traders hold on to investment positions for long periods, anticipating the investments to appreciate. The periods can extend from weeks to months. In that regard, position traders are less concerned with short-term changes in price movements.

Position traders follow trends, believing that once a pattern starts, it is likely to continue. As such, position traders incline toward obtaining the bulk of a trend's move, which would generate profit in their investment capital.

Position traders use both fundamental and technical analysis to help in making trading decisions. They also depend on macroeconomic influences, old trends, and overall market movements to get to their anticipated end.

For a trader to have success in position trading, the trader has to know the entry or exit points and have a strategy to mitigate risk mainly by placing stop-loss orders.

Who Are The Main Participants?

The online FOREX brokers create a credit line with a bank that is involved in the trade to enable access to currencies for trade. Today, investors are more rigorous and seek to diversify their trading portfolios to draw more returns.

The FOREX trade is in the financial market together with stock trading and others. However, it is different from the other trades in the financial market, such that you do not need to use a centralized exchange that has only one price for a particular currency, at a given time. It is made up of different dealers that have different rates, making the market overwhelming, but amazing because it has so many choices. Competition between the many dealers is fierce, and getting the best deal is something that happens all the time. Another good thing about FOREX is that you can trade anywhere; you are not restricted to certain markets like in the case of stock trading.

At the top of the market, the ladder is interbank, which is composed of the world largest banks and some of the smaller banks. Traders at this level trade with each other directly through Reuters Dealing or the Electronic Brokerage Services (EBS). From the interbank going down the ladder, next is the hedge funds, retail market makers, and corporations; this group does its transactions through commercial banks. Therefore their rates are higher than those of interbank. At the lower part of the ladder are the retail traders, who include individuals who are small scale traders.

FOREX trading is one of the trades that bring earning to a country; the more the responsible traders a country has, the more it earns from the exchange. Entry in this form of trade is always a good choice of investment, as there are no commissions of trading like the other forms of trade. There are no government fees, exchange or clearing fees. There are also no brokerage fees as most brokers are compensated through the "spread." The only cost incurred is the transaction fee, which is low; it ranges from 0.07% to 0.1 where the lowest is for larger transactions. The FOREX trade also has no limit like in the case of stock and features, your size of the trade is determined by the amount of money you have for investment in the trade. The FOREX is a 24-hour market; it does not wait for opening time or bell and does not depend on the day of the week or month. Which makes it suitable for all people, including part-time traders? The market also attracts everyone because of its easy entry; when compared to other financial market trades, FOREX requires a minimum of $25 and allows individuals to have mini and micro-accounts for trading. The market welcomes all people, but no individual, institution, or company can control the market price, because it is so huge. This form of trade has high liquidity because the market is so huge and accessible that anytime you want to buy or sell; there is always someone willing to exchange.

Other Financial Institutions

Generally speaking, financial institutions still control the trading volume in the foreign exchange market, accounting for 51% of the total trading volume in April 2016.

1. Non-reporting banks

Non-reporting banks are generally small banks or local banks. They are customers of large foreign exchange trading banks but do not participate in the market. Non-reporting banks accounted for about 22% of the world's foreign exchange transactions in April 2016, down 2 percentage points from April 2013.The decline in the share of non-reporting banks is mainly due to the decline in their share of spot transactions, followed by the decline in the share of foreign exchange swap business.

- **Institutional investors**

Institutional investors (such as insurance companies and pension funds) have further increased their share of foreign exchange transactions, with their share of foreign exchange transactions rising from 11% in 2013 to 16% in 2016.The increase in foreign exchange trading volume of institutional investors is mainly attributed to foreign exchange swap business. In April

2016, the daily average exchange volume of institutional investors reached 278 billion US dollars, up 79% from 2013.

- **Hedge funds and private trading companies**

Hedge funds and private trading companies (hedge funds and PTF) are also the main bodies of speculative currency trading in the foreign exchange market. However, compared with 2013, the foreign exchange trading volume of hedge funds and private trading companies decreased from 11% to 8% in 2016.They control a large amount of customer funds and can invest them in the foreign exchange market, thus affecting the transaction price.

- **Government departments**

The central bank (or other monetary management institutions) is the main government sector involved in the foreign exchange market, whose main purpose is to carry out management functions and deepen economic policies. By buying and selling currency in the foreign exchange market, the central bank adjusts the supply and demand of funds in the foreign exchange market, and then adjusts the exchange rate and foreign exchange reserves to achieve the purpose of management functions. For example, when the demand for some foreign exchange in the foreign exchange market exceeds the supply, leading to a decline in the exchange rate of the local currency, the central bank can buy the local currency and discard the foreign currency to maintain the exchange rate at a certain level.

- **Other**

For example, foreign exchange brokers who facilitate foreign exchange transactions. Foreign exchange brokers do not buy and sell foreign exchange themselves, but only connect foreign exchange buyers and sellers to facilitate transactions and collect commissions from them.

Non-financial customers

In addition, there are also some non-financial customers of enterprises or individuals, who are often participants in non-speculative foreign exchange markets. They need to exchange currencies through the foreign exchange market so that they can carry out import and export trade or investment. This part of the transaction may affect the route of international trade flow, thus having a certain impact on the price of currency in the foreign exchange market. However, compared with speculative currency transactions, its influence is limited due to its limited quantity. In April 2016, non-financial customers accounted for only 7% of the world's foreign exchange transactions.

Currency trading in the foreign exchange market has many similarities with stock trading and futures trading, for example, the three have the same objectives, and all three transactions hope to gain profits from the price changes of the subject matter. If a trader buys Facebook shares, he certainly hopes that Facebook's share price will rise in order to make a profit. By the same token, if a trader buys US dollars, he definitely hopes that the US dollar will appreciate in order to benefit from it. However, compared with financial markets such as stock trading and futures trading, the foreign exchange market has some unique characteristics, such as trading time, trading scale, etc.

Currency trading in the foreign exchange market has many similarities with stock trading and futures trading.

When Is Forex Market Open?

When trading, one currency is exchanged with another, for instance, when you exchange the Dollars with the Euros, you say you are trading Dollars for Euros. The earning comes in when the money you traded with fluctuates in value over time. The rule is always, buy when it is low, and sell when it is high. However, it is not easy to determine how low is low and how high is high; to determine the low and high therefore one needs know the factors influencing the rate of the currency in order to predict the rate of the currency in the future. The difference between the rate of selling and that of buying a currency is known as the "spread" and it is expressed in "pips." A Pip is the smallest unit of any currency.

It is not easy to predict a market trend, and therefore are methods used to guide the prediction. These methods are the technical analysis and fundamental analysis. The fundamental analysis consists of policies put forth by a country that affects the currency. The central bank of each nation has a responsibility for the well-being of a nation, and therefore, it analyses the factors that affect the economy and make policies that improve the status of the economy. It is therefore important to look at the adjustment in the policy of the country of the currency you want to trade with and regular announcement because they are the economic indicators that bring about changes in the FOREX market. The indicators include interest rates, the GDP, consumer price index, and industrial production, among others

The technical analysis concentrates on market trends, trying to see if the current trend of the currency can reverse, and if it does, how the market will respond to the changes in the future. It looks at the history of the price of currencies and volumes traded, through reading and interpreting graphs. Mathematical tools used in making technical analysis include gaps and trends, waves, and number theory. The technical analysis uses three basic assumptions: history repeats itself, prices move in trends and market discounts everything.

For one to have a reasonable profit from the FOREX trading it is good to have a good risk management plan. However, the management should be based on capital preservation; remember that you cannot trade without funds in your account. Making big profits is not bad, but it is good to have a calculated risk. It is better to have a little success rate than to risk much and lose it all.

An investor should also have a trading plan to make sure that he or she achieves the set goals. The plan should not just be written down, it should be followed just the way you plan to buy household items; always buy when the prices are low and when your prediction about the rising of prices has a higher chance of being true. And sell when your prediction that the price might fall as a high probability that it will happen. There is no proper action to FOREX trading; it is having a good plan that is based on good analysis.

Chapter 2 Forex Terminology

As with most specialized areas, the Forex market comes with its own terminology that can be utterly undecipherable to the uninitiated. Before we discuss how to trade in Forex, let's get you acquainted with those words and phrases to help you navigate the information more easily.

Ask Price: This is the price that a seller is willing to accept for a trade on the market.

Spread: This is the difference between the bid and ask price and is where the broker makes their money. The more volatility in the market, the wider the spread is likely to be.

Exchange Rate: A familiar term for vacationers, this refers to the value of one currency in terms of another. For instance, how many Euros you would get for one Australian dollar.

Currency Pairs: The Forex market does not deal with individual currencies, but with pairs of them. For example, U.S. dollar combined with the Canadian dollar. Some are much more widely traded than others.

Cross Currency: A trade in which neither of the given currency is the $ U.S. dollar.

Cross Rate: A currency exchange rate between two stipulated currencies in which neither of them are the known official currency of the specific state in which that rate is given. For instance, if an American publication quoted an exchange rate for the Canadian dollar and Japanese yen.

G7 and G20: These seven countries – the United States, Italy, Japan, France, Germany, Canada and the United Kingdom – are the countries with the most major economic developments and represent over two thirds of the world's wealth. Their currencies are stable, creating currency pairings that have high volume and volatility. The G20 includes these countries but also others including China, India, Argentina, Australia, South Africa, South Korea, Mexico, Saudi Arabia, Turkey, Brazil and the European Union. These together make up four fifths of the world's trade and 85 percent of the gross domestic product on the planet. These currencies are the ones you will focus on as a trader.

Restricted Currencies: Some governments do not allow trading or speculation with their currencies. This can be because there is a limited availability, concern about the effect of speculation or a desire to control foreign investment.

Pip: This refers to the smallest possible increment by which a currency can move in price. Some currencies are quoted to four or five decimal places, so a pip refers to 0.0001 or 0.00001 of that pound, franc or Euro. Others are quoted only to two decimal places, so a pip is 0.01.

Volume: In Forex trading, this refers to the number of units being traded at one time. One currency may only have five or ten transactions taking place on it over the course of a day, while another may have thousands upon thousands. The former therefore has a low volume of trade, while the latter has a high volume.

Volatility: This refers simply to how much change there is in the trading price of a currency over time. The most that price changes, the more volatile that currency is said to be.

Margin: If you don't have enough money to invest in a trade, you can get a secured loan from your broker to increase your capital. This is known as using margin. Doing so involves a great deal of risk as, if the trade is not successful, you will find yourself in significant debt.

Margin call: This term refers to your broker requiring you to settle your account, usually when a trade reaches a certain level of risk.

Advantages of forex trading

- **High liquidity**

Forex trading has very high cash. Getting in and out of the trade is relatively easy. You will not need to pay a massive premium on it

Low barriers to entry

Anyone can open a forex trading account. You don't need to be a high net worth individual to have a forex trading account.

- **Better risk management**

Compared to other business, forex trading has better risk management. You are in a position of managing your risk. Let us say you have a small capital of about $500 if you are thinking of just risking one percent of your money, and you can play Nano lots. You have no transaction cost all you need is to pay the spreads; this allows you to even risk five dollars on trade. Thus, helping you manage your risk better.

- **Trade anytime you want**

Forex trading is open 24/5 so you can trade anytime that you wish to from Monday to Friday. So, the market is accessible when you wake up or when you are sleeping. The choice is yours throughout the day and night to choose the best time to trade. All you need is to know whether you are a long term or short-term trader. This you can test by what is called a "pillow test" if you can put a position and go to bed at night and have a good night's sleep, then you are trading on the proper side. However, if you can put your pillow in position and you can't lie on it because you have to be on the screen watching the trader all the time, you will realize that you are trading too much or you are risking too much. Either your trade heights are too large, or your stop loses are too far, and you know that loses is something you don't want to take however with this, you are prone to making high loses. If you can put on a trade and be comfortable or walk away from the computer, you are trading the right style.

- **Simple underlying concept**

Forex trading is based on simple underlying concepts. This trade is just comparing the relative values to currencies. When you are trading forex, you are using a pair of currencies. An example is the EUR/USD. You will just think about which one of the two currencies will gain strength and buy and sell based on that. All you will need is to study the strength of any of the paired currency and make sure that you sell the currencies to make a profit or before it pulls back. This is just straight forward as compared to other things like agriculture.

- **Tradable the same as stock or futures using technical analysis**

Technical analysis is the trick when it comes to forex trading. Yes, you can use fundamental analysis as well but technical widely used by many people in the world because of its simplicity. You will only wait for the price indicators to direct you on when to enter the market and when it is time to put a stop. Something that other businesses won't do. These patterns are built by fractal geometry, and you only need your mind to make that simple move of entering and stopping once you are done with the analysis. However, to get the best, you also need to know if you are a fundamental or a technical trader. Ask yourself if you love looking at charts, different indicators. Most traders will find that they work on the technical side that is they will be looking more into the charts and various indicators as compared to the number that will be working with fundamentals. Whichever one you choose is all upon your personality; however, you need to work with that one that seems to be the best.

- **Superior leverage**

With forex trading, you will be able to control a large number of assets with a relatively small commitment of capital. As a trader, you need to make leverage your friend. Leverage is like fire. You need to learn how to make fire, and at the same time, you also need to learn how to use it wisely so that you do not burn yourself. Fire will warm the cave and cook your meet and also keep your predator's way. However, the light will also destroy all your possessions. Leverage is like fire; all you need is to use it on balance. Thus, you need to employ some severe money management tips.

To make the best in your trading, make sure that you avoid the mistakes that have been mentioned above. Again, invest more and more in yourself. Make learning a habit to improve your trade to the next level.

The Challenges Involved in Trading Forex

First, when a high amount of leverage is allowed in the forex market by the banks, dealers, and brokers, traders can be able to control large positions of forex market even with their little money. As a trader, you must first begin by understanding the use of leverage as well as the risks introduced by leverage in your account. Many dealers have unexpectedly become insolvent due to extreme amounts of leverage. Secondly, in order to trade currencies productively, it is advisable that you must first be able to have a deeper understanding of the fundamentals and indicators used in economics. Particularly, in this era, as a trader, you must have the big picture in mind. You must be able to understand the economies of other countries (especially major economic powerhouses) and how these economies are interconnected. This is the only effective way that will enable you to drive currency values and be productive.

Chapter 3 Forex Markets

With central banks, retail forex brokers, commercial corporations, commercial banks, hedge funds, individual investors, and investment management firms participating in the forex market, it is easy to see why this market is larger than equity and futures markets combined.

Placing a trade in the forex market is quite simple. The basics of Forex Trading are very similar to the mechanics of other financial markets, such as the stock market. Therefore, traders with prior experience in any type of financial market should be able to understand Forex Trading quite quickly.

Basics of the Forex Market

The FX market is a global network of brokers and computers from around the world; therefore, no single market exchange dominates this market. These brokers are also market makers and often post bid and ask prices for currency pairs, which are often different from the most competitive bid in the FX market.

On a more basic level, the foreign exchange market consists of two levels, i.e., the over-the-counter market and the interbank market. The OTC market is where individual traders execute trades through brokers and online platforms. The interbank market, on the other hand, is where large banking institutions trade currencies on behalf of clients or for purposes of balance sheet adjustments and hedging.

The backyard trade advertise (Forex, FX, or money showcase) is a global decentralized or over-the-counter (OTC) exhibit for the exchanging of monetary standards. This market decides backyard change charges for each cash. It comprises all parts of purchasing, selling, and buying and selling financial standards at present or decided costs. As far as replacing volume, it is via a lengthy shot the biggest market on the planet, trailed by means of the Credit advertise.

The Foreign Exchange Market is the place the clients and merchants are related with the deal and acquisition of faraway monetary standards. As it were, the financial varieties of a range of countries are bought and is regarded as a remote trade market.

The shape of the outside exchange market consists of countrywide banks, commercial enterprise banks, dealers, exporters and shippers, workers, financial specialists, voyagers. These are the foremost gamers of the outdoor market; their role and spot are seemed in the figure beneath.

At the base of a pyramid are the actual customers and retailers of the backyard monetary requirements exporters, shippers, vacationer, speculators, and migrants. They are true customers of the economic standards and approach business banks to get it.

The business banks are the second most sizable organ of the far-off change showcase. The banks managing in far flung exchange assume a job of "showcase producers", as in the quote every day the backyard trade quotes for buying and selling of the faraway financial standards. Additionally, they work as clearing houses, in this manner supporting in clearing out the contrast between the pastime for and the stockpile of financial forms. These banks buy the financial varieties from the professionals and offer it to the purchasers.

The 1/3 layer of a pyramid establishes the far-flung trade specialists. These representatives work as a connection between the countrywide financial institution and the business banks and furthermore between the actual purchasers and commercial enterprise banks. They are the sizeable wellspring of market data. These are surely the humans who do not purchase the outdoor money, but instead strike an arrangement between the purchaser and the vender on a fee premise.

The country wide financial institution of any nation is the summit physique in the association of the exchange showcase. They fill in as the loan specialist of the last resort and the caretaker of outside change of the nation. The country wide bank has the capacity to control and manipulate the outdoor trade promote to assure that it works in the equipped design. One of the substantial factors of the country wide financial institution is to counteract the forceful vacillations in the remote alternate showcase, if important, by direct mediation. Mediation through promoting the cash when it is exaggerated and getting it when it will in familiar be underestimated.

Hours of Operation

The FX market is a 24-hour market, from Monday morning to Friday afternoon in Asia and New York, respectively. Essentially, unlike markets such as commodities, bonds, and equities that close for a while, the forex market does not close even at night. However, there are exceptions. Some currencies for emerging markets, for example, close for a short while during the trading day.

The Currency Giants

By far, the US dollar is the biggest player in Forex Trading, making up approximately 85% of all forex trades. The second most traded currency is the euro, which makes up close to 39% of all currency trades, while the Japanese yen comes in at third place with 19% of all currency trades.

The reason that these figures do not total 100% is that every forex transaction involves two currencies. Citigroup and JPMorgan Chase and Co. were the biggest participants in the FX market in 2018, according to a study conducted by Greenwich Associates. Actually, these two banks commanded more than 30% of the global forex market share.

Goldman Sachs, Deutsche Bank, and UBS made up the remaining top five places. According to a settlement and processing group known as CLS, the daily trading volume in January last year was more than $1.8 trillion.

This is a testament to just how popular, and massive Forex Trading is around the world.

Origins of the Forex Market

Up until the First World War, countries based their currencies on precious metals like silver and gold. This system, however, collapsed, and the Bretton Woods agreement became the basis of currencies after the Second World War. This agreement led to the creation of three international organizations to oversee economic activities across the world.

These organizations were the General Agreement on Tariffs and Trade, the International Monetary Fund, and the International Bank for Reconstruction and Development. In addition to creating these international organizations, the agreement adopted the US dollar as the peg for international currencies, instead of gold.

In return, the US government had to back up dollar supplies with an equivalent amount or value of gold reserves. This system, however, ended in 1971 when Richard Nixon, the US president at the time, suspended the US dollar's convertibility into gold. Nowadays, currencies can pick their own peg, and the forces of demand and supply determine their value.

Chapter 4 What a Beginner Needs to Know About Forex Trading

Forex trading is an avenue that is making people earn a more significant income. There are many platforms where you can put that little penny in the trading and amerce that profits. However it needs you to be that wise speculator who knows who reads the indicator promptly and knows the point to make that trading. Remember that forex trading is all about the trading of currencies. Therefore you have to be knowledgeable about how the different currencies perform. The following are the basics where a beginner should know.

You should first be interested in knowing how the currencies behave in the market. That is where one ought to recognize the values of different currencies. The major currencies traded across the globe shows significant value in the market. Some of these currencies include the Us Dollar, Sterling Pound, Swiss Franc, Japanese Yen and the Euro. That is not to say that other currencies are not traded but this one has the commanding value in the forex exchange. Therefore it requires the broker and the trader to be updated on the value of the stated monies. This is because at some instances the currencies may deteriorate and increase their worth significantly. Another thing to contemplate is how the paired currencies behave with each other. For example in the forex chart you may see the Us Dollar \combine with the Euro or any other pair.

Another thing you ought to know is the type of indicators available and how one can make trading. These indicators follow specific movement criteria. First and foremost before knowing that indicator thinks of the scales used in the chart. The chart represents a graphical diagram with both the independent and the depend scales. The independent scales are normally plotted on the horizontal axis and the dependent scale on the vertical axis. Therefore, you have to know the different variables in the trading. Some of these variables are the price movement, the volume, and many others. Check on this charts ad test the movement of these variables appropriately.

Concerning the indicators, you should be aware of how these indicators behave. They are of different types and are influenced by the variables you use. For a beginner it is essential to have that knowledge of how they behave is crucial. You have to know the different types of these indicators so that you can follow their trend.

Think of the indicators like the Moving Average Convergence and Divergence. This indicator measures the two exponential moving averages. There is the Bollinger band indicator that measures the standard deviation those currencies of the currencies. Some terms like the volatility market you also need to know them. Remember that the volatility of the currency is its behavior to have either a sharp increase or decrease in the market. That is where you can either gain a sizable profit or loss.

That is not to forget the relative strength index which is beneficial for ascertaining the overbought and the oversold. These indicators are very many in particular, but when you have their information is nothing that should stop you from earning. Even the types of charts like the candlesticks. Line charts and bar charts should be at your fingertips. There are different charts for every level of your trading. For example in your case as the beginner, you can use thence stick or the basic charts.

Another thing is the trend analysis. You should analyze the direction which the indicator flows whenever you make a trade. That should help you in analyzing the peak times and recession periods of a paired currency. You also can anticipate the next performance of the paired currency if you are experienced in reading the behaviors of the indicators. You still use this information to know the right point of the market entry and the exits of the point. Those brokers who analyze the trend accordingly and are in a position of obtaining a sizeable return.

Which qualities make you as the beginner successful in the trading.

After knowing the basic you do not just start trading when you have the minimal qualities required in this business. You will realize how you will get frustrated when you stake a lot of cash then the trading fails. At other junctures you need to apply essential speculation tactics. That is the knowledge of probability and analyzing the statistics for you to stand a chance in trading. Some of these qualities are.

Be that guy who is good in decision making. Remember that the facility needs intelligence and critical thinking. You may find yourself succeeding a lot in particular segment of trading. However not to realize that it may be a trap where even after making sublime returns you will eventually gain a hefty loss. Some other times you need not consider only short term profit but fight for long-term returns. You may identify a promising venture but where whose returns are realized in long term basis. However if you are that person who needs quick money you will not be patient on that venture but look for short term profits. Moreover those who take time in making a decision realizes a pattern trend and makes the right move.

Be that risk-taker who do not fear to make a loss. If all people were risk-averse then there would no forex trading. Hey, remember that this business is like a gamble. Am sure that many people do not like hearing this term, but whenever you are dealing with uncertainties you are gambling. No matter what you do you have to sacrifice that penny expecting two possibilities which are either a win or a loss? Even other renowned investors cite that 'you have to stake big to win big'. Therefore be a risk-taker who stakes big and hopes for massive earnings of returns. Even if you fail seldom, do not give up but eventually you will win.

Persistent is another quality required for you beginners in the forex trading. When you are persistent you normally are tolerant. You never give up hope even after failing many times. Why your needs are learning from mistakes. Do not repeat the same strategy that you did which failed you. Be that person who sees the failure as a lesson to improve their ways of staking. Adopt a trial and error strategy which will eventually give you a winning edge. You do not expect keep winning all the time, you will undoubtedly lose in some instances. You will realize you will keep developing tactics of trading with this trial and error strategy. You will too familiarize yourself with the trend analysis. Therefore what is stopping you know to make that currencies trade.

Timing is also operational in the business. You have to flexible enough to identify a profitable opportunity. The way the currencies behave is like a pendulum that goes in every direction. You can use a stopwatch and identify the specific time the trading signals a return and risks or an entry point or an exit point. Those seconds or minutes you waste may be the advent of your failure. Do a demo trade which you do not have to input some cash. Look at the behavior of the currency and how they react in any substantial change. You may identify the correct timing when you need to stake. Therefore you will have that confidence to stake your money in the trading.

Intelligent speculation is required for this job. This trading requires you to be wise in reading the trends. Statistics and probability of knowledge are also needed. Those brokers are reputable in making the wise traders are the one who clearly predicts the next behavior of the trading. Their experience in reading the scales and indicators further enhances effective trading. Intelligence speculation is a skill which is learned by various strategies. One of that strategy is the trial and error method where you will consequently have that experience of trend analysis. Knowledge of the different currencies, charts and indicators gives you that winning margin. Lastly, you can consult specialists to train you about the analyzing of the currency trading.

Adequate preparation is needed in this exercise. How best can you be in a particular exercise if you are not that fully prepared? You must be that person who is willing to set your record straight. Efficient preparation starts with the person who keeps the trading records and is able to analyze the performance of the currencies using them. Always appreciate the usage of the demo account which you practices the trading. In this, you are not fearful of losing your cash. Once you are used to frequent rehearsals you are comfortable with making the trading.

What are the steps for a beginner in trading?

First, you have to have good preparations first. Trading does not fall on the moon however you need to have the gadgets for trading. You need to have that electronic device, it can be either your phone, laptop, eye pad or any other gadget. Make sure you have the best source of the internet because you need to make many references to the currencies from the network. Make sure you are comfortably sat and good to go.

Choose the best agency company in forex trading. Remember there are many companies online that broke those currencies. To get such firms one to conduct an extensive study of them. You also need to consider if they are registered and licensed. Moreover consider their brokerage fee and their essential features. It should have the necessary charts, variables and indicators which must satisfy the trader. Consult other traders to recommend you the best brokerage firm.

When you are satisfied with this create an account with them. Assess of they provide a demo account which is necessary for the trading rehearsal.

The demo account is very vital for you to practice the trading. Remember you cannot put your money in a venture that you do not know, therefore you must understand it first. If you are satisfied with it then start the trading program. The good thing with demo account is that you are not afraid of any risks since you have not staked any cash. Check at the trading platform and its chart.

Open the chart or the diagram and try to choose the currency pair. Most of the times the currencies are found in the top of the graph, its sides or the below graph. Look at the available currencies and think about them. You have to be keen in choosing the pair. You can even research how the values of different currencies and how they behave with each other. Do not forget to check their volatility and how they fair when traded. Choose those pairs and fix them at the graph.

Then choose the indicators you like. Indicators are of different types and it is upon you the trader to examine which you will understand. You can either use the Moving Average Convergence and Divergence which measure the exponential averages. You may think of the Bollinger band in the standard deviation or the RSI which identifies the overbought or the oversold. If you cannot understand them ask an expert to teach you.

Place the order if you feel you are ready for that trade. Prioritize of price as the main element in harnessing a profit of the currencies. With the currencies, pairs evaluate how the indicators move. They may move in different direction or together. You have to know the peak time and the recession times. When the waves are on higher point that is the peak period and when they are low then that is the lower period. Make your value and see the behavior and you will realize whether it is a return or loss. If the pair discourages you choose another and repeat the same action. That is until you are convinced of the best pair of trading.

Do much practice with that demo and you will realize a trend. Therefore conduct an effective trend analysis that should help you to predict the exact behavior of the pair currency. You will also know the point to amerce greater profit and big losses. Still the trend analysis will help you to identify the specific points where you can make an exit of the trade with a profit.

When you are satisfied with that demo you can stake the amount and follow the following procedures. Be accurate and persistent and try many times even if you fail.

- **Real FX Trading steps**
- **Pick a cash pair**

Choose which money pair you want to exchange. With greater than sixty five cash sets to browse, picking a replacing possibility that is without delay for you is significant.

City Index's specialized and primary research apparatuses can enable you to spot cash changing possibilities to go well with your changing style. We prescribe that you take as an awful lot time as is wished to be aware of the measure of price unpredictability associated with the money pair to assist deal with your hazard.

- **Settle on the sort of FX change**

There are three unique approaches to exchange Forex with

(a)   City Index Spread Betting
(b)   The CFD
(c) The Forex Trading. Everyone has its precise stake size:

• In unfold wagering you alternate pounds per factor development

• In CFD changing you alternate a quantity of CFDs in the unit of the base cash (money on the left). For instance, on the off danger that you change GBP/USD, your stake would be in Pounds, whilst in USD/JPY your stake would be in US Dollars

• In Forex exchanging you purchase parts in the unit of the base money (cash on the left)

• For model, on the off hazard that you alternate GBP/USD your stake would be in Pounds, whilst in USD/JPY your stake would be in US Dollars (the base stake dimension is 1000)

• **Choose to buy or promote**

When you have picked a market, you have to understand the present fee it is replacing at which you can do by means of elevating a request ticket on the stage. All Forex is stated as far as one money versus another. Every money pair has a 'base' money and a 'quote' money. The base cash is the cash on the left of the money pair, and the declaration cash is on the right. Basically, when changing faraway financial standards, you would:

Purchase a cash pair in the event that typically, the base cash would fortify towards the declaration cash, or the statement money will debilitate in opposition to the base money.

Your advantages will ascend in accordance with each enlargement in the trade cost.

Each fall in the exchange price under your open level will net you a deficit.

SELL a cash pair on the off danger that you accepted that the base money would debilitate in an incentive in opposition to the declaration cash, or the statement money will strengthen towards the base cash.

Your advantages will ascend in accordance with each point the exchange cost falls.

Each enlargement in the exchange price over your open level will net you a shortfall.

- **Spread** - FX units have two costs.

The fundamental fee is the selling cost (known as the offer), and the subsequent price is the purchase cost (otherwise known as the offer). The difference that exists between the buy price and the selling fee is recognised as the spread; and is the price of the exchange.

- **Including orders**

A request is a practise to consequently trade at a point later on when prices arrive at a specific stage foreordained by means of you. You can use stop and limit requests to help warrant that you lock in any advantages and restrict your hazard when your man or woman benefit or misfortune hazard aims come.

While now not obligatory, given the unpredictability in FX markets, utilising and appreciation risk the executive's instruments, for example, stop-misfortune requests is fundamental.

A cease misfortune request is an education to finish off an exchange at a fee extra horrible than the present market degree, and as the title recommends, is utilized to assist limit misfortunes. There are two kinds of stop-misfortune orders - popular and ensured.

A standard quit misfortune request, as soon as activated, shuts the exchange at the nice available cost. There is a hazard, in consequence that the stop value ought to be no longer pretty equal as the request degree if market fees hole.

An ensured quit misfortune be that as it may, for which a little top class is charged upon the trigger, assures to shut your exchange at the cease misfortune level you have decided, paying little admire to any market gapping.

A breaking point request is a preparation to finish off a trade at a price that is gold standard to the current market degree, and is utilized to help lock in value targets.

Standard cease misfortunes and farthest factor requests are allowed to put, and can be achieved in the managing ticket when you ahead of all your exchanges, and you can likewise join requests to present open positions.

- **Screen and close your exchange**

When open, your exchange's benefit and misfortune will currently exchange with each cross in the market cost.

You can song market costs, see your hidden benefit/misfortune replace continuously, be a part of requests to open positions and encompass new exchanges or close current exchanges from your PC or software on your cell smartphone and tablet.

- **Shutting your trade**

When you are prepared to shut your exchange, you have to do something contrary to the major exchange. Assuming you purchased three CFDs to open, you would promote three CFDs to close. By shutting the exchange, your net open advantage and deficit will be stated and shortly mirrored in your file cash balance.

Note that City Index Spread Betting and CFD archives are FIFO.

Chapter 5 Currency Pairs

On stock exchanges, you trade stocks. On Forex, you trade currency, but the currency is always traded in pairs. It would be as if you had to own some stock, but if you were betting on Apple, you had to bet against Microsoft as well. On Forex, currencies are paired one against another such as the Euro against the U.S. Dollar, or the Australian Dollar against the Japanese Yen. Getting familiar with currency pairs and how they are displayed on the Forex markets is the first step in making your way around and understanding what you are doing.

Currency Pair Basics

A currency pair is listed with an abbreviation for the currency some of the most popular currencies include:

- USD: United States Dollar

- EUR: Euro

- JPY: Japanese Yen

- GBP: Great British Pound

- CHF: Swiss Franc

- CAD: Canadian Dollar

- AUD: Australian Dollar

- NZD: New Zealand Dollar

- MXN: Mexican Peso

- RUB: Russian Rubles

- CNY: China Yuan

- SGD: Singapore Dollar

Some currencies also go by nicknames. These include:

- USD: Greenback

- GBP: Cable or Sterling

- AUD: Aussie

- NZD: Kiwi

- CAD: Looney

- EUR: Chunnel

- CHF: Swiss

You should learn what the nicknames of the currencies are or have them referenced so that if you are in discussions about Forex or reading message boards, you have an idea of what people are talking about. If you are wondering where some of these strange names came from, some of them are historical. For example, in the early days of currency trading, undersea cables were used for electronic means of communication between Britain and the United States. That's where the name "cable" came from.

The Majors

Another important concept you need to know about is the *majors.* As you might guess, the majors are the currencies used by the major world economies. However, actually, the majors are expressed in pairs and they represent the most frequently traded currency pairs. The US Dollar is involved in something like 88% of all Forex trades and so more than $4 trillion per day of the currency trading on Forex involves the US Dollar.

The majors are:

- EUR/USD
- USD/JPY
- GBP/USD
- AUD/USD
- USD/CHF
- NZD/USD

- USD/CAD

These seven majors represent 85% of all currency trading. Notice that the United States Dollar is involved in every single one of the major currency pairs. The fact that these pairs represent most of the trading is important because that means that's where you are going to find the most liquidity. That could be significant if you are looking to exit a trade quickly. To complete a trade, you've got to find someone on the other end of it, willing to buy or sell as the case may be.

Many currencies from developing or third world countries are known as "exotics." While the majors are where most of the liquidity is, that doesn't mean you can't profit by trading exotics.

Currency pairs that aren't quoted against US Dollars are called cross-currency pairs. Each currency other than the US Dollar has its own set of cross currency pairs. All currencies trade against one another, but you can consider cross currency pairs just between the majors. For the Euro you have:

- EUR/GBP
- EUR/AUD

- EUR/NZD
- EUR/CAD
- EUR/CHF
- EUR/JPY

Since there are seven majors, all major currencies other than the US Dollar has six cross currency pairs with the other majors.

Currency Pairs Are Expressed in the Same Manner at All Times

You will notice that the currency pairs have one currency that comes first followed by the second currency. These are never changed so, if you are buying Euros and selling dollars, it's EUR/USD and if you are selling Euros and buying dollars, it's still EUR/USD. The first member of a pair is called the *primary* or the *base* currency and the second member of the pair is called the *secondary*, or the *counter* currency. This is just due to historical factors and for labeling purposes, it has nothing do with one currency's relation to the other in the modern world. In centuries past, the GBP was stronger than the US Dollar and so the currency pair has GBP listed first.

Note that on futures markets, the USD is always the secondary or counter currency. That doesn't just mean when the USD is in the currency pair, on the futures markets the USD is always the counter currency so while you'll see USD/JPY on the spot market, you'll see JPY/USD on the futures market. Again, when we are talking about Forex trading in this book, we are talking about the spot market. However, it's important to be aware of what you are looking at in case you happen to come across currency pairs from the futures markets.

Let's run through a few examples.

EUR/USD: The primary is the Euro, the secondary is the US Dollar.

USD/JPY: The primary is the US Dollar; the counter currency is the Japanese Yen.

MXN/JPY: The primary is the Mexican Peso, the secondary (or counter currency) is the Japanese Yen.

The Essence of Currency Pairs

Forex trading boils down to a competition between different currencies. You are trading one against the other and one is going to rise and one is going to fall. When you are using your trading platform, you're going to see listings of currency pairs displayed. EUR/USD is pitting the Euro against the US Dollar and you're betting for one and against the other. Of course, you're not guessing or using "hope," as a Forex trader you're studying the trends and sentiment in the market, using indicators and maybe paying some attention to macroeconomic news in order to make an educated forecast. That doesn't mean it's going to be right of course.

Let's see how this works. Remember that the pairs are always listed in the same order, so you'll have to understand what kind of trade you want to enter in order to pick one currency over the other.

Sticking with EUR/USD, let's say that you believe the Euro is going to rise against the dollar. That means that you're going to want to buy Euros and use your dollars to do it. After that, you hope that when you will sell your Euros, later on, you will get more dollars back than you had originally.

To bet on the Euro for EUR/USD – you are going to *buy* this currency pair. This means you believe the Euro is going to rise and the dollar is going to fall. Remember, everything in Forex is relative. Hence, that means we're saying that the Euro is going to rise compared to the USD. Let's look at some more examples to get some practice with this.

Consider USD/JPY. If you believe that the USD is going to rise and the Japanese Yen is going to fall relative to the dollar, then you will buy this currency pair.

If you believe the Mexican Peso is going to rise relative to the Japanese Yen, then you are going to buy the currency pair MXN/JPY.

Now, remember that the currency pairs are always listed in the same way. Otherwise, if you believe the USD is going to rise against the Euro, how is the transaction going to take place? In that case, you will *sell* the EUR/USD currency pair. Let's say this again:

Selling the EUR/USD currency pair means that you are betting that the USD is going to rise and the Euro is going to fall. When you sell this currency pair, you are selling Euros to buy dollars. Yes, it's confusing, because you probably think that you don't own any Euros. It doesn't matter; the broker/dealer is going to take care of everything for you automatically.

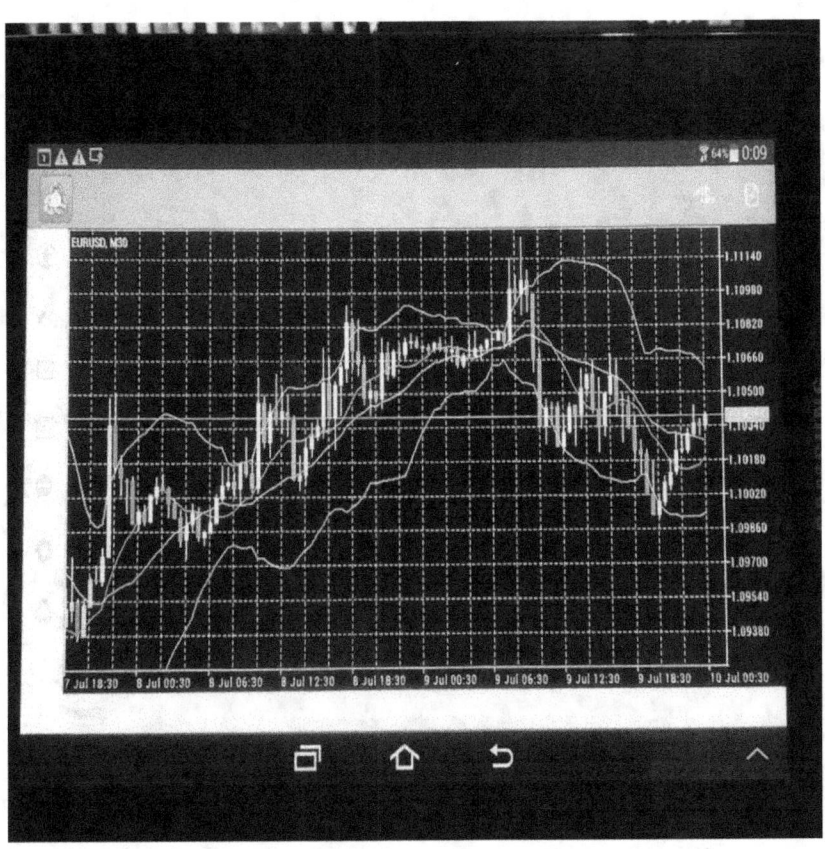

Chapter 6 Trading strategies

In this chapter, we will introduce you to some of the top Forex Trading strategies which will help you to make a lot of profit with your Forex Trading endeavors. More specifically, this chapter will help you to understand the main three methods top Forex Traders use, especially in the beginning to see amazing results when it comes to gaining profit from the trade. The primary 3 include breakout strategy, moving average crossover strategy (MACS), and carry trade strategy (CTS). As you know, there are many participants in the Forex Trading industry. Some of them don't know what they're talking about, where else other are well-versed in this trading industry. After speaking with a lot of professional who have done very well in Forex Trading, we come to you with the top three strategies which will help you to perhaps take your forex trading to the next level. The top Forex traders in the industry, have tried many approaches and have seen success with some and seen extreme failures with others.

Nonetheless, we will guide you with the top three strategies that will help you to see results from the get-go. It is very important for people starting Forex Trading to see results right off the bat, the reason why is because it will help you to build confidence with your Forex Trading Endeavors. It is essential to see quick results with for trading primarily in the beginning so that the Traders can feel a lot better about their skills. However, do not get carried away with their was also you see in the beginning. If you think you are thus hot shot in trading, news flash for you you're not. You make a big mistake if you keep using the strategies for the wrong reasons, it is essential that uses approach for the right purposes and the right cause. Which is what we're going to teach you in this chapter, so you can finally see the money grow in your bank account. Keep in mind, the initial strategies are very similar to each other as they are trying to follow a trend. The last one tries to gain profit from the interest-rate differentials instead of the market situation. People that don't know what trends are, they are necessarily a way for people to determine how the market is going to proceed with the movement on given the overall status.

The trend is essentially a way for the traders to go by the signal rather than actual facts about it, similar to technical analysis which is going by the direction. The good news is that following strategies which require you to look at Trends, can yield you amazing results when it comes to gaining profits. However there are a number of challenges to it, the first one would be it is not easy to consistently stick with it. You have to realize that friends come and go, and the game you'll get from following a strategy which requires you to look at the trends will be short-lived however can he'll do a lot of profit that will help you in the long run. Second drawback of the strategy would be that large friends can be very infrequent, again you have to realize that Trends don't come and go that easy which is why they're called Trends as they come rarely. Keeping that in mind you have to understand that whenever you see a trend, it will be short-lived and it will not happen again in a long time. Third drawback of following a strategy which requires you to look at trends, will not be as frequent. If you're looking for things are strategies which will help you with Trends then think again as it will not yield you a lot of results in the long run since trends are so hard to find. Understanding this concept will help you to prepare your mindset when it comes to the following protocol, which requires you to use patterns. Even though Trends can be hard to find, once you do find it and act on it correctly then the success rate will be very high. One thing to remember with any protocols but you require you to look at the trends, would be that you will need a lot of money to use a properly. With that being said, let's talk about the three strategies which can help you tremendously to make a ton of money with Forex Trading.

- **Breakout**

Breakout trend is a trend that you need to act on quickly to see amazing results, simply explain to you what a Breakout trend is it is when the market has suddenly gone up or down which could result in a new direction. Think of the breakout Trend as something which is just coming out, and you're guessing that it is going to be fantastic for currency there for you invest in it, most of the time it works amazingly. The only downfall will be that the breakout trend has no guarantee if it's going to turn into a trend or not. However, the great thing about the breakout trend is that you can come out of it as soon as possible. If you're full daytime trader, then you will know when the trading is going down, or the dollar is going up or down. Based on that judgment, you can pull out the money or keep going if the trend is going up or down. The great thing about the break out method would be that the market moves beyond the boundaries, meaning that you will achieve most likely new highs or new lows. Most of the time it is new highs, if there are a Currency Change chances are there is going to be a breakout. However, this isn't the case most of the time, so make sure before you get into the break out a method that you know for sure that it is going to go up. There is no sure way to find out that it is going to go up or not, however, based on your judgment and after some research, you should have a clear idea on how this trend is going to end up. Keeping that in mind, the breakout method could be an excellent way for beginners to start making some money as soon as possible. Many top forex traders recommend that beginner start with this trend, in our opinion it is a little bit on the risky side. However, any trend is going to be risky, and Forex Trading, in general, is dangerous as compared to having a full-time job.

- **Carry out trade**

The carry trade method is not something many beginners follow. However it can be used by beginners to see amazing results. The way the special words as they bank on currencies dropping down and up. For example, a great carry out trade with be the Canadian and US dollar, the US dollar has always been high. However, there have been times when the Canadian dollar drops down very low and vice versa. When that happens, you know that you could trade your money and make more back depending on where you live. Many people have banked on the Canadian and US dollar to make this work for them in terms of profit. The great thing about the carry out method is that it is very calculated. However, it is based on trends are requires you to let your money sit for a long time. There are a lot of other ways to do the carry out trade. However, we will keep it very simple for you so you can understand how to follow the carryout trade indeed and see the most benefit out of it. Keep in mind that the carryout rate is perhaps the safest trend-based method you can use to make more money. Overall, the only downfall with the carryout trade would be that you have to let your money sit for a long. Of time as compared to the break out method. However, once you do get the idea of how it is to be followed, you will be in a much better position and terms of making more money even if it is in the longer term.

- **Moving average crossover**

It applies the use of simple moving averages (SMA) - an indicator which lags and utilizes data of older prices unlike other strategies, also tends to move at a slow rate than other ones. The longer the time averaged to the SMA, the slower the rate of movement. Often, top traders tend to use longer SMA with some shorter SMA. To explain to you how it works is that it looks at the lower prices and determines whether the new rates will be higher or not. This strategy is solely based on the trading system. If you are not getting better trading strategies, then chances are you will not see the results you are expecting from this method.

- **Research**

Regardless of the investment that you make, be sure always to do your research. Doing research is a must. It is what will increase your chances of making the right investment decision. As the saying goes, "Knowledge is power." The more that you understand something, the more likely that you will be able to predict how it will move in the market. This is why doing research is essential. It will allow you to know if something is worth investing in or not. Remember that you are dealing with a continuously moving market, so it is only right that you keep yourself updated with the latest developments and changes, and the way to do this is by doing research.

Just because you have surfed the web for a few hours does not mean that you are already in the position to make an investment decision. You should understand that doing research should be part of your daily life as an investor/trader. Even if you are just a side trader, it is still essential that you do your research so that you will be informed of the best trading practices.

Remember that gaining information is not limited to just surfing the web for information. It is also suggested that you join online groups and forums that are related to your chosen investment. This way, you will be able to meet and connect with like-minded people. There is also a good chance that you can learn something from them.

Do not rush the process of doing research. Take note that you make decisions based on the information that you have on hand, and such information that you have will depend on the time and efforts that you put into doing research. Make sure that all of your decisions are backed up by solid research and analysis.

- **Write a Journal**

Although not a requirement, writing a journal can be beneficial. You do not need to be a professional writer to write a memoir; however, you need to do two things: Update your journal regularly and be completely honest with everything that you write in your journal. By having a journal, you will be able to identify your strengths and weaknesses more effectively. It can also help you realize lessons that you might otherwise overlook.

You can record anything in your journal that is related to your business or investment. Ideally, it should contain your reasons, as well as your objectives. You can also write down your mistakes and new learnings that you encounter along the way.

In the first few weeks, you might not appreciate the value of keeping a journal. However, after some time, you will start to understand its importance, especially once you begin to notice your progress or developments. The important thing is to persist in writing your journal. It will allow you to view yourself from a new perspective, from a standpoint that is free from bias and prejudice.

- **Have a Plan**

Whether you are going to start forex trading or trade in general, it is always good to have a plan. Make sure to set a clear direction for yourself. This is also an excellent way to avoid being controlled by your emotions or becoming greedy. You should have a short-term plan and a long-term plan. You should also be ready for any form of contingency. Of course, it is impossible to be prepared for everything. If you are suddenly faced with an unexpected and challenging situation, take your time to study the situation and develop a new plan. Never take action without proper planning. Poor planning leads to poor execution but having a good idea usually ends up favorably. You should stick to your plan. However, there are certain instances when you may have to abandon your project, such as when you realize that sticking to the same program will not lead to a desirable outcome or in case you find a much better idea. Proper planning can give you a sense of direction and ensure the success of execution.

Make your plans practical and reasonable. Remember that you ought to stick to whatever project you come up with, so be sure to keep your ideas real. Before you come up with an idea, you must first have quality information. Again, this is why doing research is very important.

What if you fail to execute your plan? This is not uncommon. If this happens to you, relax and think about what made you fail to stick to your plan? Was it favorable to you or not? Take some time to analyze the situation and learn as much as you can from it. Indeed, having a plan is different from executing it. It is more challenging to implement a plan as it demands that you take positive actions.

- **Learn from Your Competitors**

Pay attention to your competitors and learn from them. Studying your competitors is also an excellent way to identify your strengths and weaknesses. You can learn a great deal from your competitors, especially ideas on how you can better improve your business.

Your competitors can also help you promote your trading goals and draw more techniques. This way, you get a better idea of how to trade. You do not have to fight against your competitors; you can work together.

It is prevalent for people online to support one another. , it is a good practice that you connect with other traders, especially those who are in the same niche. Do not think of them as your direct competitors, and you might be surprised just how friendly they can be.

Now, a common mistake is to consider yourself always better than the others. This is wrong as you are only deluding yourself, making you fail to see the bigger picture. Instead of still seeing yourself better than your competitors, learn from them, and see how you can use this knowledge to improve your trading endeavors

- **Cash-out**

Some people who trade forex or invest in crypto currency commit the mistake of not making a withdrawal. The reason why they do not cash out is so that they can grow their funds. Since you can only earn a percentage of what you are trading/investing, having more funds in your account means that you can make a higher profit return. Although this may seem reasonable, it is not a recommended approach. It is strongly advised that you should request a withdrawal. You should understand that the only way to truly enjoy your profits is by turning them into cash; otherwise, it is only as if you were using a demo account. Also, by making a withdrawal, you get to lower your risks, since the funds that you withdraw will no longer be exposed to risks. You do not have to remove all your profits right away. If you want, you can withdraw 30% of your total profits, allowing the remaining 70% to add up to the funds in your account. The important thing is to make a withdrawal still now and then.

- **Take a Break and Have Fun**

Making money online can be fun and exciting; however, it can also be a tiring journey. Therefore, give yourself a chance to take a break from time to time. When you take a break, do not spend that time thinking about your online business. Instead, you should spend it to relax your body and clear your mind. If you do this, then you will be more able to function more effectively. This is an excellent time to go on a vacation with your

family or friends or at least enjoy a movie night at home. Do something fun that will put your mind off of business for a while. Do not worry; after this short break, and you are expected to work even more.

Making money online is a long journey, so enjoy it. Making money online can be lots of fun. Do not just connect with people to build a good following, but also try to make friends with your connections. You do not have to take things too seriously. Keep it fun and exciting.

Chapter 7 More Strategies
Channel Breakout

These are the trends that will break out of the resistance and support curve, and often, they show up after a new event, or a piece of news is released. This is where you will want to bring in your knowledge of the economy so that you can determine when a breakout is going to occur. If you guess correctly, you can get into the market before the price goes up and sell when it reaches its top. Or you can get out of the market in time if the news is bad or brings up uncertainty before the market crashes and you lose out on all your money.

Many traders find that working with a technical analysis can be a great option to help them earn a good amount of money on the Forex market. It does require looking at a lot of charts and graphs to see success. But for those who can learn about the trends that occur with a specific currency, and who are willing to watch out for some big news items that may change the course of their currency pair away from its historical values, then a technical analysis may be the right option for you.

Fibonacci Indicators And Applying Them

There are ways to understand in case your currency trading strategy is excellent or successful.

• Start knowing how effective it has been in the past. It will pay to learn simply how much previous or current users associated with the operational system have received so far by utilizing the strategy. Regardless of that, additionally obtain some informative data on how much is the drawdown that is maximum of system in its previous trading.

• There was a win-loss ratio which it is possible to check. It is about how much you have won compared with much you have actually lost. Apart from that, there is also a profit-loss ratio. This s about the average winning trade set alongside the trade that is losing.

• You would also need to know how consistent the system is in delivering earnings.

Horizontal Levels And The 'Swing Points'

This is going to involve liberal use of math, so you should be prepared. Actually, here is the perfect moment to add in a little advice. If you are not comfortable with pips and lots, then don't jump in on a trade. Try to familiarize yourself with these terms and the way they work. This is because when you finally start trading, you should be aware of the changes happening to the currency on every level. With that small recommendation, let us move on.

I am going to use the fourth decimal point system for the example below. If you can understand it, then you can apply the same calculation to a five-decimal-point system as well.

We have now established that EUR/USD shifted from 1.1183 to 1.1184. Therefore, currently, EUR/USD = 1.1184 or in other words, 1 EUR to 1.1184 USD. We represent this as 1 EUR/1.1184 USD.

We simply have to replace the above components with values.

We know for certain the following: The amount of change in the value of the counter currency is 0.0001 USD. The rate of exchange is 1 EUR/1.1184 USD.

In the end, we are looking at the following value:

[0.0001 USD] × [1 EUR/1.1184 USD]

We can shift the values around so that the equation looks like the following:

[0.0001 USD/1.1184 USD] × 1 EUR

This gives us the following value:

0.00008941344 EUR

The above value of the euro is what you get for every one unit that you trade.

Now let us assume that you have chosen to pick up a mini-lot of 10,000 units of the EUR/USD. When there is a single change of pip in the exchange rate of the currencies, then the entire change in the value would be 10,000 units × 0.00008941344 EUR. This would give us roughly 0.89 EUR change in the position of the value of the currency exchange.

Of course, the keyword to remember is "roughly" as every time the exchange rate shifts, so does the value of each pip.

The above example is just a simple explanation of the way pips work. When you are working with the forex market, you might have to make a note of the values in order to make the best trade.

Trendline Trading

This procedure can form the basis of a Forex strategy that can be used on any time frame that suits you. At a minimum, you need to have two dips for an upward trend or two peaks for a downward trend. Once you have drawn the trendline, you wait for the price to touch the trend line a third time. You can buy 2-5 pips above a high point or sell 2-5 pips below a low point.

Cci Moving Average Strategy

You can use the CCI oscillator for the same purpose. With a CCI moving average strategy, you will use two exponential moving averages together with the CCI oscillator. Typically, a 7-period exponential moving average and a 14-period exponential moving average are used. To enter a selling position, you look for a crossover, of the 7-period moving average to move below the 14-period moving average. Don't make a move immediately; you want to make sure that there is not going to be a rally that reverses the trend lines a second time. If the downtrend is confirmed, look for overbought conditions in the CCI. If you see overbought conditions, then it's a good time to sell a currency pair. For buying conditions, you will look for the formation of an upward trend. The first signal is going to be the 7-period exponential moving average crossing above the 14-period exponential average. Check the CCI for oversold conditions, and when you see that and confirm that there is not going to be a resumption of the downtrend, you buy your currency pair. This is good to use with the majors. You should also incorporate candlestick analysis to confirm your signals.

Bollinger Band Trading Strategy

Bollinger bands are a tool available on any trading platform. They provide you with a wealth of information, including a dynamic estimate of support and resistance. This is done using a 20-period moving average, which will display as the "middle" Bollinger band. The standard deviation, one above and one below (or many people use two standard deviation widths) form the upper and lower Bollinger bands. If the trend of the middle band is upward, then this is a buy signal. If the trend is downward, this is a selling signal. When you add Bollinger bands to a chart, you are going to see the price fluctuating about the middle Bollinger band, and going near (or slightly exceeding) the upper and lower Bollinger bands which mark out current levels of price support and resistance. To make a move, if the trend is upward and the price comes back and touches the middle Bollinger band, then buy your currency pair. On a downtrend, if the price rises back to touch the middle Bollinger band, then this is your sell signal.

Gartley Fibonacci Patterns

A Gartley pattern is a tool used to look for a retracement. This is when a temporary, and relatively small reversal happens before the overall trend resumes. What you want to look for as a pattern forming on the price chart that resembles the letter M. So the price will rise up, then drop down but not all the way down to the previous price level, rise up again, and drop down again. It's not going to be an ideal "M" shape, but instead, it will probably come up not quite as high on the second peak, and the last point is going to be higher than the first point on the far left. Wait for the pattern to appear on the chart. Then you want to check the candlestick patterns and see if there is a bullish reversal signal. Then you want to buy a currency pair at a price level that is 2 pips higher than the high price of the most recent bullish candlestick. To protect yourself in the event of a reversal, you can put a 5 pip stop loss order below the last closing price of the final bearish candlestick.

When using this technique to sell a currency pair, you look for the same setup but look for a bearish reversal pattern. Then you look to sell at 2 pips below the low price of the most recent bearish candlestick, and buy if the price goes 2-5 pips above the last high price seen in the chart.

The Floor Trader Strategy

The floor trading method is primarily a swing trading strategy, but it can be used for day trading as well. If you plan to use the floor trader strategy, you will rely on 9 periods, and 18-period exponential moving averages, and look for the 9-period moving average to cross below the 18-period moving average to signal a downtrend, and hence give a sell signal. Alternatively, you will look for the 9-period moving average to cross above the 18-period moving average to indicate an uptrend, which will be a signal to buy a currency pair. Then wait for a few candlesticks to pass to confirm that the trend is holding and that the candlesticks are showing no signs of reversal. Then you want to wait for a retracement before entering the trade. In a downtrend, this will allow you to sell at a relatively high price because a retracement is a temporary move upward in price before it resumes the longer-term downtrend.

Now let's consider the opposite situation. That is, we are going to look at an upward trend in price. This time, a retracement is doing to be a small drop in price before the trend resumes. So when the lines cross with the short-term moving average going above the long-term moving average, then you look for three candlesticks to go by to confirm that the trend is not going to reverse. Then wait for the retracement, and buy when the price dips to the relatively low.

The time frame depends on your time frame as a trader. So the candlesticks could be one-minute candlesticks if you are scalping, or 1 hour or even 1-day candlesticks if you are swing or position trading.

Supertrends

Supertrend is an indicator that you can use on your charts, combining trend information with volatility data.

Using this strategy, you will use two exponential moving averages. These will be the five-period exponential moving average, and the 20-period exponential moving average. As usual, you want to look for cross overs. When the five-period moving average crosses above the 20-period moving average, this is an indicator that an uptrend is coming.

Conversely, when the five-period moving average moves below the 20-period moving average, this tells us that a downtrend is coming. Then you want to combine this signal with the supertrend indicator. The supertrend indicator is going to be color-coded, either green or red. If it turns green and you see the five-period moving average crossing to the upside, this is a buying signal, so you will want to buy your currency pair at this point.

On the other hand, if the five-period moving average crosses below the 20-period moving average, and the super trend indicator turns red, this is a sell signal. Therefore, if you see this signal, then you will sell your currency pair. Super trends are very popular among Forex traders.

Hull Moving Average

The Hull moving average is a more sophisticated moving average. Like the exponential moving average, it uses price weighting to give more weight to recent prices when it computes the moving average. It is a surprisingly accurate moving average, and it will give you a nice smooth curve that seems to pass right through the centers of the candlesticks on your chart. If you want, you can use the Hull moving average in place of the exponential moving average for any strategy, but this type of strategy seems to work best when you are using one-day candlesticks. So it's going to be best suited for swing and position traders (or end of day traders as well) when looking for points to enter and exit your positions.

The strategy is the same as with other moving averages. That is, you are going to want to look for points, where a short period moving average crosses a moving average that has a longer period. If you are looking into a swing or position trading strategy, you are going to want to use longer periods. As an aside, when you use the longer periods the Hull moving average is not going to fit through the middles of the candlesticks, that happens for a nine period or less moving average.

For this case, using the Hull moving average for a longer time frame, you are going to want to set up a 50-period Hull moving average and an 80-period Hull moving average. The idea here is to look for the usual crossings and confirm by checking for reversal signals in the candlesticks.

Let's consider a buy signal first. Looking for a buy signal, there has been some sort of downtrend. You are keeping your eye open for the 50-period moving average to cross above the 80-period moving average. When it does so, then you are going to want to look at the candlesticks. If you see an uptrend or bullish signal in your candlesticks, then this is a definite signal to buy a currency pair.

Now consider that the currency pair A/B has been in an uptrend. You may have either bought the currency pair A/B, and you are looking for the right time to close your trade by selling it. Alternatively, you could be looking for an opportunity to sell to open the A/B currency pair, so that you can bet on currency B against currency A.

The first thing you are going to look for is the crossing over of the lines. When you are in an uptrend, you should be seeing the short period moving average above the long-term moving average. When it crosses below, this is when you get ready to either close your position, if you had previously bought the A/B currency pair, or you are looking to sell to open. Either way, confirm the signal by checking the candlesticks. If it confirms that downtrend has been starting, then you can go ahead and make your move.

The Hull moving average method is not restricted to longer-term trading. You can use a shorter-term scenario with the Hull moving average. For example, if you are intraday trading, you could use a 9 period Hull moving average and a 20 period Hull moving average with 5-minute candlesticks.

Which Daily Routine Strategies To Use

There are many daily routine strategies for a Forex trader to choose from. The specific daily routine strategies used are not exclusive. So if you are trendline trading, that doesn't mean you couldn't also use other strategies. However, some people do tend to stick to one trading strategy, rather than mixing them up.

The first step in becoming an effective Forex trader is to focus on one and only one overarching strategy. By overarching strategy, I mean that you first focus on the main time frame that you are going to use for your trades. Are you going to be a scalper, an intraday trader, or a swing trader? This is the type of question that I am talking about in the present context. This is the first and most important question to settle in your mind.

Beginning traders should stick to one overarching strategy and one only. Later, when you get more experienced, you might want to try other methods. So you might start off using swing trading, and after you have a few months of experience under your belt, if you have the time available to do it, then you can consider trying out scalping at that time. In fact, many experienced traders are going to have one main style of trading they use, but they will dabble in other styles from time to time.

But beginning traders should stick to one style because you are going to end up with your head spinning around, if you try mastering multiple styles simultaneously. The best method for novices, in my humble opinion, is to use either end of day trading or swing trading. These trading methods do require a little bit of patience, but the advantage of these methods is that they are slower paced. If you try scalping, as a beginner it's going to be like being in a pressure cooker. This is going to cause you to make mistakes, and also you are going to get overwhelmed by emotions that will lead you to make many bad decisions. When we are talking about trading, we are talking about bad decisions leading to lost money.

So it's better to start off with a slower trading method that doesn't require you to be at your computer constantly, making split-second decisions. That type of trading style is best left for the experts. You can transition to that type of trading style after you have learned the methods through experience.

Now, what about the daily routine strategies considered in this chapter. It is true that some strategies might be better suited for one style or another. But the main thing behind these strategies is that they are actually pretty general in application. The main things we are looking for with the strategies is to spot a price reversal, which can give a buy or a sell signal. This can be done using all of the strategies listed here, except the trendline strategy.

While it's possible to pick and choose many strategies to use, it is probably better to stick to one or two strategies. First of all, any Forex trader needs to have a firm grasp on candlestick charts, and you need to be able to spot reversal patterns in the candlesticks on sight. So your first step in preparing to be a successful trader is to learn the candlesticks. There are many books and online courses that cover candlesticks in-depth, I suggest that you seek these out and really learn candlesticks from top to bottom.

The second tool that every Forex trader needs to understand and use are the moving averages. In fact, in the vast majority of cases, candlesticks and moving averages are all that you need. The specific moving average is not really that important. However, there is one exception here. Although simple moving averages are the default on some platforms, a price-weighted moving average is better to use for more accuracy. The exponential and Hull moving averages are quite effective for this purpose.

Trend line trading is more of an art than a science. It's also not something that takes a large amount of effort. As a result, traders that are using some of the strategies that are described in this chapter, are going to use trend line trading as well, at least some of the time. Generally speaking, trend line trading is something that will be used to give you an idea of where to go with your trades. It really cannot be considered as a technical indicator.

Novice traders are going to be intrigued and excited by all the various strategies. This can turn out to be a problem. It's better to master just a small set of strategies rather than trying to master them all. So look at all of them to try them out, then settle on just a couple that you will use over the long term. Here is a fact about the strategies. Many of them actually give you the same information. So there is no point in piling on different moving averages, for example.

Now a quick word about software products. There are many software products that are available on the market to do analysis and help you make your picks. Some software products will even suggest the currency pairs for you to trade. The software can automate all of the analysis that is done, and it will give you buy and sell signals. Since it can scan dozens of currency pairs in a matter of seconds or minutes, it can find currency pairs that are trending for you, so that you don't have to put time into doing this.

If you are going to use software tools, my advice is that you still put the time and effort in to learn how to read the charts, and how to spot reversals. You should not blindly trade based on what a software tool is telling you to do. What I suggest is that you confirm what the software tool is telling you to do, and if your mini-analysis agrees with the software, then you can buy or sell as indicated.

Chapter 8 Basics of Technical Analysis

Very well, you have just completed the part dedicated to the basics of online trading so you are fully able to start studying the principles of technical analysis.

We will cover topics of fundamental importance such as the main market theories, technical indicators, graphic configurations and much more.

What the Technical Analysis of A Market is

Technical analysis is the study of the behavior of financial market prices through the use of statistical tools and its ultimate purpose is to predict the future price trend.

This type of approach differs from other types of analysis, such as fundamental analysis, because it argues that price movement is the result of a set of human factors reflected by the movement of market prices.

The primary objective of technical analysis is to identify the levels of entry and exit from the market and thanks to a series of increasingly sophisticated tools, the trader can evaluate which are the most convenient inputs.

Technical analysis uses two tools that allow traders to analyze a market:

• *Technical indicators*: statistical tools that give us different information on price trends;

• *Graphic tools*: these are tools that allow you to draw directly on the chart.

Of course, in order to be able to technically analyze a graph, we need analysis software; there are several types, both free and paid. Personally, I suggest you use Metatrader, a completely free trading platform that has nothing to envy to paid platforms.

Thanks to these two tools, added to the personal knowledge of the trader, we can successfully analyze the trend of a financial chart and start to determine the levels of purchase/sale.

The three fundamental principles of technical analysis

Technical analysis is a very large and complex subject but it is based on three fundamental principles.

1. *The price discount everything*: the first principle of technical analysis indicates that the price movement fully reflects all the

information available on the market. For this reason, it is not strictly necessary to be aware of all the existing news as they are already present and reflected on the market.

2. *Prices are moved for trends*: the price movement is never completely random but follows trends that alternate with their second market clicks. The objective of the technical analysis is to define these trends and interpret them to identify potential points of inversion of the trend.

3. *History repeats itself*: the movement of prices, in addition to following trends, is repeated over time. This is possible because the subjects that act on the market are always the same and the latter tend to alternate moments of euphoria with moments of confusion. These attitudes of the subjects cause particular movements that form the so-called price patterns, very useful for predicting the future price trend.

The Dow Theory

Most of all we know of technical analysis is attributed to the studies of the American journalist Charles Dow thanks to his theories of market analysis published in the Wall Street Journal at the beginning of the 20th century.

The Dow theory we are going to analyze in this article was also the main point of reference for many analysts such as Gann or Elliot and although it is a theory dated more than a century ago, it still remains current and functional.

According to Charles Dow, prices do not move according to criteria of randomness but have a directionality (trend) that can be expected with a good chance of success. Dow also demonstrates how market trends are similar to tidal wave movements advancing and cyclically retreating until force runs outgoing from high tide to low tide, just as trends continue with ups and downs to their own inversion.

All of Dow's articles on price movements are contained in what will be called Dow theory summarized in six rules.

1 - The price discounts everything

According to Dow, in fact, the price reflects perfectly all the information known so all that we need for proper analysis is already contained in the chart.

2 - The market is made up of three trends

The Dow Theory identifies three main trends in a market: primary trend, secondary trend, and minor trend. These three trends differ from one another mainly over the duration, in fact, the primary trend can last even more than a year, the secondary trend has an intermediate duration that can go from three to six months, while the minor trend is characterized by movements that do not they usually exceed thirty days.

3 - The trends are divided into three phases

After deciding on the three market trends, Dow divides every trend into three further phases. The study of these three phases will make you understand the main dynamics of a market and how and why prices move.

1. *Accumulation Phase*: During the first phase, the formation of a trend begins. This is the moment when the few subjects with direct access to information enter the market and buy at particularly advantageous conditions.

At this stage, the market still continues to move sideways as the vast majority of traders have no knowledge of what is happening.

2. *Participation Phase*: At the beginning of the second phase, called participation, prices start to rise and even less informed individuals enter the market. This combined intervention by investors will push the price higher and higher until the bullish momentum is going to run out. The participation phase is the real trend with high volumes of exchange and high liquidity.

3. *Distribution Phase*: In the third and last phase, ie when the price has gone upwards beyond its limits, the most informed subjects realize that it is time to close their positions and sell at very advantageous prices. At this moment the inversion of the trend begins and this causes a real panic among the investors causing a race to the bottom.

4 - The indices must confirm each other's

To formulate this principle, Charles Dow made explicit reference to the American railway and industrial index, supporting a direct correlation between the two. Basically, Dow notes that the two indices have a high positive correlation and that any reversal of the primary trend must be found in both to confirm.

5 - Volumes must confirm trends

Volumes are one of the most important aspects of a financial market, in fact not only are they often able to anticipate the beginning of a new trend but they also give us confirmation of the current trend. Dow says that the trend must be accompanied by an expansion of volumes. In fact, volume tends to increase in moments of trend and decrease in moments when the market moves sideways.

6 - A Trend remains valid until a signal appears to confirm the inversion

This fifth principle of the Dow theory really is very important and it should always be kept in mind when we trade in the same direction of the trend as with the trend following strategies.

In fact, a trend remains so until a clear inversion signal appears on the graph. The greatest difficulty consists in understanding in advance whether we are facing a real inversion of the trend or a simple price correction.

Support And Resistance Levels

The levels of support and resistance are to be considered as the first important element that a trader must identify on the graph before starting any type of analysis.

These are important levels of the chart in the vicinity of which the price tends to assume a particular behavior and they occur when we are in a substantial balance between the forces pushing upwards and those pushing downwards.

To fully understand the concept of supports and resistances in trading, we must imagine the level of support as a floor and the resistance as a roof of a multi-storey building.

These two levels will be true for those who live, for example, on the first floor of the building, but if we go up one floor, the first resistance will become new support and we will have a new resistance above our head.

Remember that you always have to see the market as a continuous struggle between bulls (buyers) and bears (sellers), the former try to push the price up, while the latter try to push it down. This vision will allow you to understand very well the next market dynamics.

Support levels

The support level is that level in which a price that is falling tends to stop its descent and to bounce upwards. In this case, we have a selling force, the bears, which pushes the price down until the latter is considered too low to continue to fall further and finally rebounds upwards. This is because the bulls realize that the price has reached an advantageous level to buy and they cause, with their long orders, a price rebound.

Always remember that a level of support is valid until it is violated on the downside and becomes a resistance, just like the example of the building we have done before.

Resistance levels

Resistance, on the other hand, is the price level of the graph in the vicinity of which the price stops its bullish run and rebounds downwards. Opposite the support level, in this case, the bears intervene as soon as they realize that the price has become too high, they sell and bring down the price.

As for the supports, also the resistances remain valid until the price will violate them on the rise making them become successive supports.

Static and dynamic supports and resistance

The support and resistance lines can be of two types: static or dynamic. Substantially only the position and how they are drawn change. Very often it also happens that the price finds support or resistance not on the same level but along the diagonals, in this case, we talk about supports and dynamic resistances.

The main difference between dynamic and static supports and resistances is the fact that in dynamic lines the price level varies over time and is therefore delineated by an oblique rather than horizontal line, otherwise it is in both cases graph levels that hinder the natural price run.

Rules of tracing support and resistance levels

Now let's see what rules you need to keep in mind to properly track support and resistance levels whether they are static or dynamic.

1. The lines must combine at least two minimums or maximum prices and the more points of contact, the greater the reliability of the level of support/resistance;

2. Daily and weekly closing and opening prices represent important levels of support/resistance;

3. If a level of support is violated, it becomes a future resistance; in the same way, if resistance is violated, it becomes a future support as in the example of the apartment;

4. The higher the timeframe used, the greater the importance of the support/resistance level. Therefore, for the price it will be easier to violate a support or resistance on the timeframe rather than on the weekly timeframe;

These rules define standard and important rules to keep in mind when at the beginning of your analysis you need to track support/resistance levels on a chart.

Chapter 9 How to Place Stop Loss

Stop-loss is one way of managing our trading risk once we enter the market. Although a few other traders can regard it as a sissy, I don't like dealing with Stop Loss. And at the end of the day, it gets me good results. It helps to keep me sticking with a well-controlled system of trading.

If we agree to use stop failure, we have to be careful when it is enforced. If the market price is so close to our stop loss, we must do nothing. Always try replacing your stop loss from the open position level at a further stage.

Replace the stop loss at only one reason: Trailing Stop Strategy (although trailing stop strategy is hardly ever used).

The question now is... where should we avoid our loss in each trade? Here are a few tips that I can give you:

1. Measure the difference between your stop loss and the rate of your open position.

Generally, I use those rules: Eur / Usd: the gap of stop loss to position open= 35 pipes Gbp / Usd: a gap of end loss to position open= 50 pips These are the total losses you can expect for each transaction. Keep that in mind, still. Without this gap law, we will not enter the market.

2. Entry strategy

Instead, with your trading system, you can predict your best entry point. And if you decide to enter the market at a certain point (using your trading strategy), don't forget to take your losses into account. Where is your stop loss put using tip #1's gap rule?

Try putting your stop loss under (long position) or above (short position) help point.

For example, we had EUR / USD support, and resistance rates are R3 1.3052 R2 1.2962 R1 1.2906 Pivot 1.2816 S1 1.2760 S2 1.2670 S3 1.2614 After calculating patterns, you find 1.2870 to be the best shortest position for yourself. In other words, the stop loss would be 1.2905 when you use the 35 gaps rule (see element #1).

Sadly, 1,2905 isn't a good stop-loss point. Why? Why? It is not limited by the level of resistance. If the market goes upwards, the technical element of your Stop Loss is not well covered. It is, therefore, very easy for the market to enter your stop loss. The nearest resistance is 1.2906, more than 1.2905. And what we're doing here is pushing our stop loss a little above 1.2905. Say we're moving it to 1.2910. Now you have a well-protected stop-loss technically.

Do not forget the rule of gap when moving Stop Loss (as stated in point 1). We must, therefore, shift our open place plan as well.

And now, the project is shortened by 1,2875 (5 pips above 1,2870) and interrupted by 1,2910 (5,2905).

3. Keep calm as you come too close to your failure on the market.

Anything could happen very quickly in Forex. When they enter the market, nobody can control people's madness. Yet' risk management' is the most important thing when coping with this mad world. Successful traders know they had to deal with lost trades often.

So let it go if your stop-loss is reached. This is just how it is.

Where to Put a Stop Loss

It is a digital "rule" of trade on the stock market to periodically be caused by a stock wherever you put your end loss, just before it continues to rise to higher levels.

This is only something to expect if you use a stop-loss. Sadly, no stop-loss asks for much larger problems, and the market likes to reward those who are stupid, lazy, or dumb, with the only reward for their actions. It does not matter if you set the top 10% or 3% from low, high, or close. You can use stops dependent on uncertainty, using Fibonacci retracing ratios, manual analysis, pivot points, the decline in percentages, or any other method. Regardless of how complex your calculations are, you will often find that you sold only for a temporary price rise that was just enough to cause a stop loss–your stop loss-for no good reason. Learn to live with it. On the other hand, and you are able to control the risk and say something about the probability of a spike ejecting you from a position. The more you stop with the recent price action, the less likely it will be. However, the more you shop, the more you will have to tolerate risk (downside price excursion). You are prepared to accept infinite threat without using a stop at all. With a "clean" stop, you can accept very little danger, but you will significantly increase the chances that a small spike will throw you out. The tighter your stop, the more expulsion spikes occur in a given period of time. The only way to solve this problem is to find the best balance between a reasonable rate of excessive expulsions and an acceptable loss due to this expulsion. In other words, the compromise which causes the least amount of pain (psychological or financial) must be found.

Magee and Edwards (Stock Trends Technical Analysis) say that a good stop based on closing prices is 3 percent below an increasing trend. The stop is only triggered when the stock closes at or below the stop. Nevertheless, if a trader intends to sell on the basis of intraday market action rather than closed markets, it implies that the stop is 6% below the upward trend. Underneath or below the last small dip is usually the best place to stop. Nevertheless, there is sometimes no recent trend or apparent slight decrease. That's when you have to use a math stop. lowest, or nearest number since purchased it or a volatility-adjusted factor stop put relative to the highest, lowest, or near point since you bought the product. As a guide for stopping, Magee and Edwards, Weinstein, Schwager, Murphy, and many others use trend lines, rises, and changing averages. Continuous patterns follow the bottom line, falls are nothing more than essential recent bottoms, and moving averages normally go somewhat below the recent bottom line. In the absence of all these, it also makes sense to use the latest highest low as a reference point for putting stops. Without a trend line or dip to use, your trailing stop may simply be 3% or 6% (or some other distance) below a moving average that follows your trends closely or even lower than the highest stock level since purchased it.

The predicted average holding time has a huge impact on the tightness of your stops. For example, for the 2.3 percent rule, the "sweet spot" is about 10 to 15 market days. The " forex trader" spectrum is only three days or less (a lot of traders concentrate on keeping periods of up to one week), and the duration is about 8 to perhaps ten weeks. The rest of the forex traders rely on the intermediate timescales. In the very short run, the 2.3% rule allows a decrease in comparison with the anticipated profit. Nonetheless, it works well when you try to lock a 4 to 10% increase in a two-week transfer. If the stock is not too "wild," it will also work well for forex s of a month or more to lock in gains of 10% to 20% or more. Nevertheless, you may have to loosen the stop for more volatile stocks and more than 15 days for daily holding periods. For example, a stop up to 6 percent below the highest level reached by the share in longer-term investments since it was purchased can be very effective. One-stop with which one of our N traders have experimented and which has proved extremely useful for intermediate trading is 4% below the lowest. When used, the whipsaw was seldom activated and did not give up much of the gain from the larger moves. It would also give up 4% or more of the smaller 8% motions. This is why some investors rely on stops 3% or less below the lowest. The compromise was the higher frequency at which an individual was unnecessarily prevented from increasing stocks. It is best to develop a personal stop-loss program that you can easily use. The predicted average holding time has a huge impact on the tightness of your stops. For example, for the 2.3 percent rule, the "sweet spot" is about 10 to 15 market days. The " forex trader" spectrum is only three days or less (a lot of traders concentrate on keeping periods of up to one week), and the duration is about 8 to perhaps ten weeks. The rest of the forex traders rely on the intermediate timescales. In the very short run, the 2.3% rule allows a decrease in comparison with the anticipated profit. Nonetheless, it works well when you try to lock a 4 to 10% increase in a two-week transfer. If the stock is not too "wild," it will also work well for forex s of a month or more to lock in gains of 10% to 20% or more. Nevertheless, you may have to loosen the stop for more volatile stocks and more than 15 days for daily holding periods. For example, a stop up to 6 percent below the highest level reached by the share in longer-term investments since it was purchased can be very effective. One-stop with which one of our N traders have experimented and which has proved extremely useful for intermediate trading is 4% below the lowest. When used, the whipsaw was seldom activated and did not give up much of the gain from the larger moves. It would also give up 4% or more of the smaller 8% motions. This is why some investors rely on stops 3% or less below the lowest. The compromise was the higher frequency at which an individual was unnecessarily prevented from increasing stocks. It is best to develop a personal stop-loss program that you can easily use.

If you want a reference point other than the lowest, the following can be of assistance. A review of all inventories of The Valuator found that the average low was 1.7466% below the average high and 1.882% below the average closure. Such data can be used to put an end to the stock's highest and lowest closure since its purchase. Therefore, if the stock rises, the stop locks further gain. This works best if the stock generates a number of new heights, each considerably higher than the previous. If the stock quickly returns to more "normal" levels, however, a 1-day spike could cause you to stop the next day. Go away from inventories that often spike. The specialist could "shot" the stock simply to take out orders for stop-loss at lower prices. In other terms, the expert momentarily lowers the stock price so that he can purchase some equities at the lower price and sell them at a slightly higher price almost immediately afterward. If looking at buying a stock that often picks up, the trader must try to stop just outside the spiking comfort zone of the specialist. If such a placement requires too much risk, you will find another stock. I prefer to focus on occasionally spiking stocks. Look at the charts and see the size and rate of descending spikes. Try to determine how much these spikes fall.

The implementation of a volatility-adjusted stop is more general than merely a percentage stop, because it adapts to the time period used by the individual "study system" (a 15-minute price bar, 30-minute price bars, daily price bars, etc.), besides adapting to the volatility. Rigid percentages neither can do but are easier to calculate for non-mathematicians. If you are attempting to measure your own losses and you have no math experience, you can use the software to calculate losses (searching for a "stop-loss method" via Google, and monitoring the trail), or simply make appropriate improvements to the 2.3 percent law. That is to say, if your stops are triggered too often before upwards movements are finished, change them to 3%, 4%, or anything. We assume, however, that the stop loss adjusted for volatility is not only more sophisticated but also more effective. Consider the following now.

You don't have to abandon the sales discipline. It's certainly your safety net, though. This saves capital if you do not pay attention to the actions of your inventory during the day. If you don't have time to rive to the grafts on the stock exchange on your computer, you need only take about 10 minutes for your positions to stop once a day (even when the market is closed) or once a week (even on weekends). You can then disregard the market until your next stop is changed. If, however, you just watch your stock and it doesn't "behave" that way, just remove the stop and sell your stock.

Don't Trade Without a Stop Loss

I do not get an invitation to go to a webinar for a little over a week to learn to trade without stops. The invitation includes warnings that traders are suffering from unnecessary losses through stops. Nothing could be more from the facts, family. Of course, you can be picked up from time to time by putting an improper stop too close to resistance or anticipated support. This is much better than being vulnerable to catastrophic loss by trading without stopping.

A stop-loss order is also an order to sell or buy a position or stock for futures or choices when the stated price is reached. When this price is attained, the stop-loss order becomes a market order, and the position is immediately liquidated at any price. The exercised value may be far from your stop price in a strong market; that is la vie. The stop loss is intended to reduce the loss in one place.

Future trade is a high-risk effort, and only a few people can make a living. For thrive, asset protection and risk management must be given the highest priority. You should not be willing to lose more than 1% of your trading assets. With such risk management, you can theoretically lose 100 consecutive trades before the game is blown out. In fact, doomsday will come a lot sooner with this record (believe me). Advantages of the Stop-Loss Order The stop-loss order is low-cost catastrophe insurance, and nothing is required. Additionally, when a trade is made, a stop-loss order allows the decision to be free of any emotional impact. The "thinking" pause is nothing but psychological inertia.

The Trailing Stop A trailing stop provides a trader with the continuous defense of his position as it is more and more competitive. Through trailing the stop loss while the prices move to the trader's advantage, a significant part of the profit is gradually covered against a sudden price reversal.

By default, stop loss placement is all about risk management and the conservation of assets. It is, therefore, necessary to always avoid using a dollar amount irrespective of the technical position indicated in the ideal map.

You need to follow one brainer; don't use a stop equal to or greater than the average time frame bar scope you exchanged. If the average range of 1-minute bar is 1.00 points, don't use a stop of 1.00 points or less and don't expect to be taken out by the "noise" of the market, for example.

Whatever you decide, the risk to the reward ratio should always be measured. Do not lose 1 point for anything under 3.00 points, i.e., a risk: reward ratio of 1:3 or better. An R: R is a sure way to the poor house with 1:2 and 1:1. Off-floor scalpers are doomed to extinction because they risk a lot for little gain with each service. In addition to the bid: ask slippage with each trade and commission costs, it is difficult overtime to go ahead.

If you want to escape the annoyance of stopping yourself by stopping sweeping, it is common sense to quit. Bringing one or two ticks beyond a new high or low is a question of being removed while attempting to fade these regions. A complete point beyond those apparent price levels is far less likely to come to a halt.

To comply with all relevant rules and regulations, please be so kind and read the following disclaimer: risk statement-past performance is not necessarily indicative of future results. In the absence of so-called "experts," The risk of loss in futures contracts for trading goods can be substantial. You should, therefore, consider carefully whether this exchange is acceptable for you in view of your circumstances and financial resources. As you know,

(1) you will experience the full loss of funds that you deposit with your broker to position yourself in the commodity futures market, and losses over and above these sums may be incurred. If the market runs counter to your advantage, your broker may be asked to invest, in short notice, a considerable amount of other margin funds to retain your position. If you do not provide the funds needed by your broker, your asset can be liquidated at a loss, and you are responsible for any shortfall arising from your account.

(2) You can find it difficult or impossible to liquidate a position under certain market conditions. For example, if the market hits a regular fluctuation price limit ("limit move"). This can occur.

(3) Placing conditional orders, such as "Stop-limit" or "stop-loss" orders, does not automatically limit losses to

the sums envisaged, because the exchange conditions under which the order is imposed can prevent the execution of such orders.

(4) This involve risk by All futures positions, and the position of "spread" might be not less risky than the position of a clear "short" or "long."

(5) The high leverage (gathering) often obtainable in futures trading due to the low margin requirements can work against both you and you. Leverage could lead to significant losses as well as gains.

(6) You must consult your broker about the existence of the protections available to safeguard your account for funds or assets.

(7) Foreign transactions include the execution and processing of foreign exchange transactions. This is valid even if the foreign exchange is officially "connected" to a domestic exchange, in which a transaction performed on one market liquidates or places itself in the other. No domestic organization, including execution, distribution, and clearance of exchange transactions, controls foreign exchange operations and no domestic regulator has the power to enforce foreign exchange regulations, and no foreign

laws. In addition, these laws or regulations can differ depending on the foreign country in which the transaction takes place. For these purposes, foreign trade consumers may not be given such protections related to domestic transactions, including the ability to use alternative domestic dispute resolution procedures. The funds received from consumers to marginalize international futures transactions, in general, cannot be provided with the same protections as the funds obtained for marginalizing potential domestic transactions. Until trading, you should know the international rules that apply to your particular transaction.

(8) Finally, the value of any foreign future or options contract and therefore the possible profit and loss resulting from it can be affected by any shift in the exchange rate between the placing of the order and the liquidation of the international futures contract or the termination or exercise of the foreign option contract.

Chapter 10 How to Read Trading Charts

A trading chart is a sequence of prices of a particular stock over a specified period in the stock market. Unlike before, up to date charts are found online. You can access them using a smartphone, tablet, iPad, laptop or desktop. They are simple at your disposal whenever you need them. The structure of a trading chart is quite simple. It has a y-axis and an x-axis. The y-axis indicates prices of securities while the x-axis indicates time intervals for the period of the chart. The prices run from left to right across the horizontal axis with figures in the farthest right indicating most recent prices. Trading charts are prepared and interpreted by specialists in the stock market who identify, analyze securities and predict their future prices within a specific period. However, you don't have to be a technical analyst to be able to read them as they are quite simple to interpret.

Prices of securities are affected by economic and non-economic factors while the chart's time frame is determined by the amount of data available for a given stock and the ease with which that data can be compressed. Time intervals can be in minutes or hours depending on the period the chart is focusing on. The data in the chart changes from time to time as new buying and selling orders enter the market while old ones are canceled and filled. There are vital data and price points found at the top of the chart. This data gives information about that particular chart, you must know what this identification data means.

Company name

This is the entity, a company or fund whose prices are being analyzed and shown in the chart.

Ticker Symbol

This is a symbol representing the company or fund being traded at that particular time.

Bid

- This is normally represented by **B**. It is the highest price a buyer is willing to buy a particular security.

Time Interval

This indicates the time the chart represents. It can be in minutes or hours.

Ask

- This is represented by **A**. It indicates the lowest price a seller is willing to sell their security.

Volume

- It is represented by **V** on the chart. This is the total number of shares being traded by the stock market in a particular season.

Last

This is the last price quoted for a certain security.

Open

- It is represented by **O**. This is the price for which the stock market has opened that day.

Previous Close

- This is represented by **PC**. It is the last closing price of the stock the previous day.

High

- It is represented as **Hi**. This is the highest price a stock has traded on that day.

Low

- Represented as **Lo**, this is the lowest price a stock has traded on that day.

Net CHG

This represents a change in price between the closing price of the previous day and the opening price for the next day. Net % CHG is that change expressed as a percentage of the total price of a particular stock.

Trading charts are classified according to the time frame they represent. These charts can be intraday, daily, weekly and monthly charts. Intraday and daily charts are used by short-term traders and investors in the stock markets. These charts illustrate the prices of stocks within various hours of the day. Weekly charts are used by those traders and investors wishing to analyze intermediate stock prices within the week. Monthly charts are designed for long-term investors and traders. They represent up to years of data for a particular stock market.

Trading charts are represented in the following ways:

- Bar charts
- Line charts

- Candlestick charts

Bar charts are the most complex among the three as they show highs and lows in addition to opening and closing prices. Line graphs have a line drawn from one closing price to another closing price. Candlesticks are the most commonly used because they're easy to read and interpret, they're nothing short of visual aids. Let us look at how these three charts are read and interpreted.

Chart Analysis

To guide you on how to correctly read and interpret a trading chart, we are going to use a sample bar chart, a real one for that matter. The chart we are going to use is that of Weatherford International, whose stocks trade in the New York Securities Exchange. The period in question is 14th September 2005 at 4.00p

There are four main stages in a stocks bar chart, namely:

- Consolidation
- Uptrend
- Another consolidation
- Downtrend

The chart above broke out of its consolidation in July and assumed an uptrend. A stock is said to be in an uptrend if it is moving forward towards the upper right corner as is the case in our sample chart. This first pullback is the best time for an investor to buy stocks otherwise they'll have to wait for the next trend. The trends then change drastically after a certain period (end of July in our case) marking the beginning of the second pullback. You can still buy stocks at this stage but it is unlikely that that particular trend will last long. If a stock does not maintain its uptrend, it gets into another consolidation before it starts falling. This continuous fall is referred to as the downtrend. The chart above can be predicted to maintain an uptrend and this makes it

worth investing in, but before we arrive at this conclusion, we need to look at the finer details in the chart.

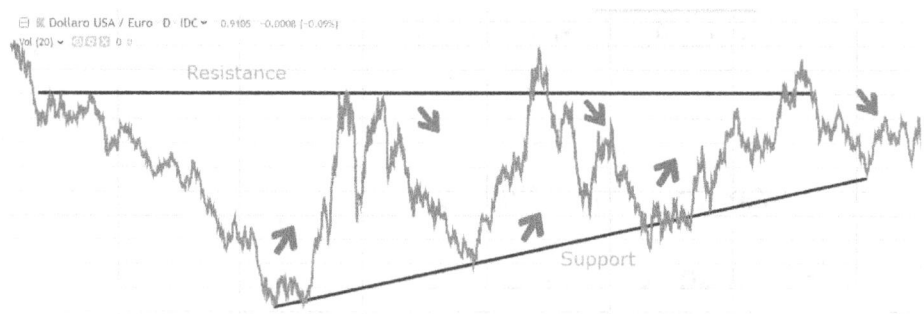

Interpreting Candlesticks

The first thing you need to look at is the price of the stock during a particular period. In our chart, various prices are represented by candlesticks in red, black and white. As the name suggests, these candlesticks are vertical rectangles with a wick extending at its top and bottom. The wick at the top represents a high while the one at the bottom represents a low. Remember the definition of these terms. The nature of the candlesticks will guide you in determining whether you're dealing with a bull market or a bear market. It will also help you study trends in the chart and make accurate predictions about future prices.

- White candles normally represent a bullish market where prices open near the low and close near the high of the period.

- Black candles are quite the opposite of white ones, they represent a bear market where prices open near the high and close near the low.

- A candlestick with a small body and long wick represents a hammer. A hammer is a pattern in the bull market that indicates an uptrend or downtrend (hanging man).

- A pricing line occurs where a long bear candle is followed by a long bull candle that opens slightly below a bear's low.

- A bullish engulfing line occurs when a small bear candle is engulfed by a bigger bull candle after a major downtrend.

- Doji and morning stars are bull market patterns that indicate indecision and imminent fall respectively.

- Spinning tops occur when the distance between open and close and that between low and high are negligible. It is an indication that the pattern is neutral.

- When smaller candles overlap on the body of a bigger candle, it causes a Harami pattern. This pattern indicates a loss of interest in a certain stock.

Smoothness

The next thing after the price that we need to look out for in this chart is its smoothness. If its trend is smooth like in our sample chart, it means that the stock is reliable and the investor is free to invest in it with confidence. A chart that is not smooth should be a red light about the behavior of that stock. You can't give a guarantee that the stocks will go up in the future.

Breakout

As a trader or investor, a breakout is another feature you must look out for while analyzing a stock chart. Breakouts happen immediately after the opening bells ring, in the middle or towards the end of the trading period. Always aim to buy a pullback as close to the breakout as possible as this is the best time to measure the level interest of a particular stock. It will put you a step ahead of someone that buys later. Traders use breakouts to decide whether to buy more of a certain stock in the future or not to buy.

Range

Moving forward, a stock that is assumed to do well in the future has a relatively wide range of candlesticks across it. A small range means that the stock is progressing in an uptrend but is struggling. Such a stock does not guarantee 100 percent safety and thus should be approached with caution.

Patterns

Patterns in the chart are something you also need to look out for though not very significant. As long as the pattern is moving up, its shape does not matter. The pattern comes in handy when we're confronted with two stocks with almost similar patterns. Always choose the one pattern you can interpret without much difficulty.

Gaps

Some stocks will exhibit gaps along the time horizon. As much as these gaps are normal, look out for abnormally many gaps in a chart as this may mean that a stock has had too many buyers already. Many gaps in a chart is an indication that many breakouts have occurred, a time when many pullbacks are bought. Investing in that kind of stock is a major gamble with two extreme outcomes. It could be a huge gain or a painful loss.

Fibonacci retracement levels

These are levels that indicate the weakness of a particular stock. A stock is considered safe if its Fibonacci retracement level is above 50%. Any level below that means that the stock is doomed and might collapse any time. Avoid investing in stocks with degenerating prices.

Tails and Shadows

These are features at the bottom of the candlesticks that indicate that the stock is getting support from financially powerful individuals and institutions. It means that you are insulated from a possible fall within that trading period. This kind of support is represented by red or green lines running below the candlesticks. A stock that gets support will jump to its previous high, thus maintaining an upward trend. From our sample graph, this trend can be seen between August and September sixth.

Volume

The volume is the total number of shares trading in a given period. A stock that has a bigger volume is doing well and many people are interested in it. Although this is a good stock to invest in, it can also turn out to be a risky investment. Too much interest in a particular stock may lead to it being overbought. Its prices will likely fall in this case. Stocks with a low volume pullback, on the other hand, are considered to be struggling. They are still worth investing in but with a lot of moderation. Every next one of its breakouts could be the last unless institutional investors come to its rescue.

Having gone through all the basics and details about trading charts, it is now time for you to familiarize yourself with as many of them as possible and interpret them accordingly. These terms and features might look scary at first but trust me, they will be second nature every next time you interact with each. You should be flexible enough to realize that the thousands of new charts you meet every day require the exact approach like this one so you shouldn't be intimidated. After a while, you will be able to prepare your charts which will be much easier to interpret compared to those that have been prepared by someone else. Lastly, keep in mind that nothing is ever certain in the stock market even with a correct analysis of the charts. The unpredictability might be caused by external factors like government policies that might come sweeping through the market like a tsunami, catching everyone unawares and causing chaos.

Chapter 11 Currency Futures And Cryptocurrencies

What Are Currency Futures?

Future contracts are standardized contracts that are exchanged on organized future markets for the required delivery date. It is generally used by MNEs as a dodging instrument.

The forward contract does not have parcel estimate and is custom-made to the need of the exporter, though the future has standardized round parts. The date of conveyance in forward contracts is debatable, while future contracts are for specific conveyance dates.

The agreement cost in forwarding contracts is based on the offer or the offer spread, while brokerage fees will be charged for the future exchange. The settlement of forwarding contracts is to be done just on the termination date, while benefits or misfortunes are paid day by day if there should be an occurrence of outcomes at the end of the exchange. Forward contracts are issued by business banks though worldwide money related markets (for instance, the Chicago Commercial Trade) or foreign trades issue future contracts.

- **Swap**

Foreign trade swap represents about 55.6 percent of the normal every day foreign trade turnover of the world, while spot bargains represent 32.6 percent and mostly forward for 11.7 percent.

Purchasing cash at a lower rate in one market for quick resale at a higher rate in another with a goal to make benefit from the disparity in return rates in various currency markets is known as currency arbitrage.

- **Options**

Foreign currency trade options provide the owner the right to buy and sell a static amount of foreign money at a pre-determined price, within a specific period. It is an agreement provided by the buyer and that gives the buyer an entitlement but not an responsibility to buy or sell financial assets at a time through a specified date.

The buyer is under no obligation to buy or sell the currency but the seller is required to fulfill their obligation. It provides flexibility for the holder of foreign currency not to buy or sell the foreign currency at pre-determined value unlike a future contract if it is not profitable for the seller.

Currency trade options, are specified in two types, call option and foreign currency options. A call option gives the buyer the right to buy the foreign currency at a pre-determined price and used as future payables. It gives the buyer the right to sell foreign currency at a pre-determined price, and it is used to verge future receivables. However, foreign currency trading options are one of the most effective tools against the exchange rate risks as they offer great flexibility than forward or future contracts because no commitment is required from the buyer under its currency options.

Remember greed is a curse. This is perhaps the perfect advice for forex traders. Any story you might have heard is either false or a pure stroke of luck. Getting greedy can cause you to risk a very big portion of your capital, so no currency trade professional would recommend it. You must not forget that no one gets rich overnight.

CRYPTOCURRENCIES

Many have wondered exactly how cryptocurrency works. Cryptocurrency is synonymous with digital currency. It is a decentralized digital coin that functions as a medium of exchange. However, since cryptocurrency is also very different from fiat currency, there is much more to how it works.

A number of the ways cryptocurrencies work are mentioned below:

Transactions: A transaction occurs whenever a cryptocurrency is transferred from a cryptocurrency owner to another via their respective digital wallets. Whenever a transaction occurs, it is automatically submitted to the blockchain, which is a decentralized public ledger where the transaction will be confirmed. After the successful completion of a transaction, it is verified with a cryptographic signature, which is an encrypted cryptography (security code) for ensuring that the transaction was initiated from a credible source.

The confirmation for a transaction processes within ten minutes. Confirmations are usually accomplished by miners. Once a transaction has been fully confirmed, it will then be added to the public ledger, where it remains for as long as the program exists. A confirmed transaction is thus permanent and can never be altered or deleted from the public ledger.

Public Ledgers: A public ledger is a list of all the transactions that have ever been confirmed and entered into a blockchain. In essence, it is a complete history of a cryptocurrency ever since its creation up to the current moment. The information stored in the public ledger is not limited to a history of transactions alone; it also includes encrypted information about the cryptocurrency owners.

Cryptographic techniques are used to ensure the accuracy of the records that are confirmed and stored in a ledger. One of the benefits of the ledger is the ease for which it can be used to check new transactions to ensure that a digital currency holder does not attempt to spend beyond the number of digital coins he or she possesses. The public ledger is considered synonymous with the term, transactions, in blockchain.

Mining: Each transaction must undergo a confirmation process before the transaction can be considered to a completed transaction that will then be recorded on a blockchain. This confirmation process is called mining. A transaction that has not yet been confirmed can never be recorded in a blockchain, and is thus not considered valid until it is confirmed. It is only after the confirmation of a completed transaction that the transaction can be added to the public ledger. Once the transaction is added to the blockchain, it becomes an irrevocable.

It is important to note that the confirmation process is not easy. It requires that the miners solve difficult computational problems or a mathematical puzzle. Each successful solution the miner makes signals that a transaction has been fully completed.

The confirmation of transactions, however, is not exclusively assigned only to some particular miners. Instead, mining is open source, and thus this offers all miners equal opportunities to solve the mathematical puzzles, and therefore confirm transactions.

When a miner has successfully solved a puzzle, he or she then updates the public ledger with a block of transactions. These updated transactions will now be kept permanently in the ledger. The miner receives a fraction of the cryptocurrency as a reward for his or her efforts. This mining process is called a proof-of-work system. This is what is responsible for a digital currency's security. The connection between the confirmed transactions, blocks, and the public ledger increases the overall security of the digital currency, thereby making it virtually impossible for an individual to alter the content of the public ledger.

Digital Wallets: Unlike the traditional hard currencies, cryptocurrencies are digital. Cryptocurrencies are thus stored in software programs, known as digital wallets, which are digital equivalents of a bank account. Transactions are made when there is a transfer of digital currency from one digital wallet to another. Without digital wallets, no transaction can occur. The recent growth of a vast majority of these coins points to the potential future value they have for everyone's lives.

WHY TRADE WITH CRYPTOCURRENCIES?

The changing perception of cryptocurrency has led to the increased application of these currencies and their use in different aspects of life. A cryptocurrency investor can perform several different kinds of transactions with their coins. Some of these transactions are:

- **Make a donation:** If one wishes to make a donation to a worthy cause or charity organization, this can be accomplished with cryptocurrency.
- **Finance an education:** Some universities around the world accept Bitcoin for tuition. The first university that accepted Bitcoin for tuition was the University of Nicosia, Cyprus. Tuition can also be paid through Bitpay, which is a payment processor with a reputation for excellence. As other universities increasingly begin accepting cryptocurrencies for tuition, it will make this process more convenient for students.
- **Crowdfunding:** When contemplating raising funds for a project, many cryptocurrency investors have now turned to cryptocurrency. Also, as an investor, one can contribute to a project by making a contribution with cryptocurrency. There are several successful projects that have been exclusively funded with digital currencies. For example, the Jamaican Bobsled team was exclusively sponsored by Dogecoin. Another project that

was financed exclusively with cryptocurrency is Lighthouse. Cryptocurrency has a bright future as a dependable source of crowdfunding.

- **Vehicle Purchase:** Tesla made the decision to accept payment with Bitcoin and sold the Tesla Model S for a whopping 91.4 Bitcoin. After this successful transaction, another car, a Lamborghini Gallardo, followed suit and was sold for an incredible 216.8 Bitcoin.
- **House Purchase:** The first home bought with digital currency was a villa sold in February, 2014, for 1,000 BTC, in Indonesia. Another home was sold in Las Vegas, Nevada, for a whopping $157,000 BTC.

These are only some of the transactions that can be made with digital currencies. As the number of cryptocurrency enthusiasts grow, the types of transactions that can be made will also increase.

HOW TO TRADE CRYPTOCURRENCIES

Investing in cryptocurrency need not be a chore; it should be viewed instead as an opportunity to see an investment grow. The following tips are designed to help investors make the best decisions when choosing which cryptocurrency to invest in and which platform, or exchange, to use:

- Never invest more than what one can afford to lose. Cryptocurrencies are volatile, fluctuate rapidly, and an investor must be ready for the risks involved. Therefore, to minimize the impact of any loss, one should only invest amounts that will not overly affect their overall finances.
- Make certain that coins are safe. An investor should choose a method of storage they trust and are comfortable with. Many investors prefer the hardware wallet option because of the freedom it offers them to be in absolute control of their currencies.
- Buy cryptocurrencies only from exchanges with excellent reputations. There are many scammers are out there who are ready to prey on the ignorance of newbie investors. Search the ratings of the exchanges first before using them, or use the list of credible exchange platforms above.

- Understand how cryptocurrencies work before investing. This means performing due diligence on these currencies before investing.
- **How to Invest**
- While one does not need to understand all the technicalities behind the operation of a cryptocurrency before becoming an investor, this does not mean it is fine just to go ahead and invest in any currency. Before investing in a cryptocurrency, one **must** perform the following:
- **Due diligence:** It is imperative to research the top cryptocurrencies to understand the investment pattern. Research should include the history, current price, rate of appreciation in recent times, and the potential for growth. One can start by researching the top cryptocurrencies discussed above.
- **Visit an exchange:** Pick one of the cryptocurrency exchange platforms from those provided above. Visit the official website of the exchange and create a personal wallet.

- **Determine how much to invest:** Despite the allure of cryptocurrencies and the hype surrounding them, many financial experts have suggested that investors in digital currencies should invest only what they can afford to lose, in the event of circumstances that cause a loss of the investment. In this case, an investor would not lose all their savings but only a portion of it.
- **Make a purchase:** After deciding on an amount to invest, go ahead and buy the currency. There are tons of trusted sellers to buy from. Contact a credible exchange where the chances of getting legitimate coins for purchase are high. Buy the coins and keep them until they appreciate. Later, if desired, sell them for a profit.

If one implements these tips to invest in a cryptocurrency, the investment process should be easy.

BEST CRYPTOCURRENCIES FOR TRADING

Cryptocurrency is an Internet invention that is quickly becoming an international sensation. While Bitcoin continues to be the front runner, thousands of other cryptocurrencies have been created to serve different purposes. Cryptocurrencies, however, are not created equal and each one can have many different features designed to make them stand out from the pack. What follows is a list of the Top Ten Cryptocurrencies that are changing the world:

- **Bitcoin**

Bitcoin is the first decentralized digital currency. It is responsible for starting the cryptocurrency revolution that eventually led to the creation of thousands of other currencies designed to meet the growing demand for digital coins. Created by Satoshi Nakamoto in 2009, Bitcoin currently has the biggest capitalization of all the digital currencies in existence. With a market value of approximately $250 billion at the time of this writing, Bitcoin dwarfs other currencies in the digital currency world.

Thus Bitcoin is considered to be the reference point, when discussing cryptocurrencies, because of its importance in relation to other cryptocurrencies. The coin has such a large reputation and value that, in relation to Bitcoin, all other coins are collectively referred to as "altcoins," in other words, alternative coins to Bitcoin. For this reason, Bitcoin always comes up whenever a list of the top cryptocurrencies is compiled.

- **Ether**

Created by a 21-year-old programmer, Vitalik Buterin, Ethereum is a decentralized platform that can be used for the execution of smart contracts. First launched in 2015, it was sold to the general public as the "next generation cryptocurrency and decentralized application platform." Currently, as of this writing, Ethereum has an impressive market capitalization of over $73 billion.

Ethereum is known in particular for its peer-to-peer smart contracts that have enabled developers to develop applications that can be used for signing contracts, while making obeisance to the terms of the contract, without a third-party in the middle.

- **Litecoin**

In 2011, a former Google employee, Charles Lee, invented Litecoin. He released the digital currency in October 2011 as another alternative to Bitcoin. Litecoin possesses some of the outstanding qualities of Bitcoin, as it can be used both as currency and a medium of exchange. As of this writing, it currently has an estimated market capitalization of $180 million and is gradually working its way to becoming one of the digital currencies that will shape the future.

- **Monero**

In 2014, Monero, an open-source digital currency was created. Monero focuses on decentralization, privacy, and scalability. This cryptocurrency can run on a wide range of Operating Systems, such as Linux, Windows, Android, and MacOS. While Monero functions on similar principles as other cryptocurrencies, this digital currency was created with the goal of improving existing digital coins by creating a more egalitarian mining process.

In 2016, the cryptocurrency experienced an unprecedented surge in its market capitalization. Its transaction volume for that year also increased tremendously as a result of the adoption of the currency by some major organizations, such as AlphaBay.

- **Ripple**

Ripple is simply one of the best cryptocurrencies on the market. Released to the cryptocurrency market in 2012 as a currency exchange, Ripple is a real-time gross settlement system and remittance network. As of this writing, Ripple currently has a market capitalization estimated to be over $76 million, after it overtook Ethereum to become one of the most sought-after cryptocurrencies. This year alone, Ripple has experienced an astounding 20,000 percent appreciation in value.

Ripple is built on a consensus ledger, internet protocol, and native cryptocurrency. It was designed to make it possible for cryptocurrency users to conduct instant and secure financial transactions with another party anywhere in the world. According to Brad Garlinghouse, Ripple Chief Executive Officer, during an interview with Bloomberg Television, "within the year of crypto, Ripple has outperformed every other digital asset out there."

As a leading cryptocurrency, some banks have integrated the cryptocurrency into their system to make payment easy for their customers. Some of the notable companies that are using Ripple are UBS, UniCredit, and Santander. Many banks and other financial institutions are increasingly adopting Ripple as a credible payment network. Two of the features of this coin that makes it acceptable for use in the banking industry are its affordable price and peerless security.

- **Dogecoin**

Dogecoin was not created as a digital currency given the potential to have any impact on people. Instead, it was created as a "joke currency," in the likeness of an Internet meme, Doge. However, the coin took off and gradually triggered the creation of an online community of users. From December 6, 2013, to January 2014, Dogecoin reached an estimated market capitalization of approximately $60 million. Currently, its capitalization is estimated to be $1 billion.

When compared with other digital currencies, the initial production schedule of Dogecoin was rapid. By mid-2015, Dogecoin had 100 billion coins in circulation. Every year since 2015, over 5.2 billion coins have been added. Dogecoin has proven useful in social media, where it is often used for tipping users that contribute noteworthy content to the Internet. Users of this digital currency believe the coin will soon experience a great increase in value, an overall rise in value of the coin that is referred to with the expression "To the moon!"

Dogecoin is also frequently used for fund raising. For instance, during the Doge4Water campaign, it raised thousands of dollars. The campaign was so successful that over 4,000 donors made donations with the coin, including an anonymous donator, who donated some 14 million Dogecoin, worth approximately $11,000 at the time of the donation.

- **Dash**

Dash is a cryptocurrency used for making instant, anonymous payments when shopping online. With Dash, purchases from office or home can be made with a direct payment from a Dash wallet. Dash can save time while shopping because the platform makes payments easy and stress-free. While the Dash platform makes payments easy, it also offers a practical way to protect financial information while shopping online. It does this by ensuring that account balances and transaction activities are all kept private. This privacy additionally helps thwart potential scammers.

Apart from the privacy offered by the platform, Dash also provides maximum security. All the transactions conducted on the platform are confirmed by a very powerful computing power, a 200 TerraHash, and the more than 4,500 servers hosted in strategic locations around the world. All these features make Dash one of the Top Ten Cryptocurrencies to consider investing in to reap many financial benefits from the cryptocurrency world. As of this writing, Dash currently has a market capitalization of approximately $4 billion.

- **MaidSafeCoin**

MaidSafeCoin is also known as Safecoin. This cryptocurrency was created by the Secure Access for Everyone (SAFE) network. SAFE is a security-oriented data platform and was created to loan out a space on your personal computer in return for coin. Safecoin is designed to ensure that at there will always be only 4.3 billion coins in circulation. These coins will also never be identical, as the coin has its own unique features and identity. A couple of decentralized apps currently depend on the SAFE network for their data storage because of the security it offers them. As of this writing, the coin has a market capitalization of approximately $40 million.

- **Lisk**

Lisk is a unique cryptocurrency, in that it is a crowdfunded digital currency and prides itself as "the first modular cryptocurrency utilizing sidechains." Lisk shares some similarities with Ethereum, such as it can also be used for developing decentralized apps. This is available for developers that are good at Javascript. The currency is useful for creating e-commerce stores, social media platforms, and other decentralized applications. Recognized as the first cryptocurrency built on sidechains technology, as of this writing, it has an estimated market capitalization of $25 million.

- **Zcash**

Zcash is another cryptocurrency that is a decentralized and open-sourced. Therefore, it offers privacy protections that cannot be easily breached. This makes it one of the most secure cryptocurrencies. The identities of parties involved in Zcash transactions are carefully concealed when transacting with Zcash, thus hiding information about the recipient, sender, as well as the value of the Zcash held on the blockchain. While

Bitcoin remains the undisputed top digital currency, these other nine cryptocurrencies are important competitors in terms of both security and privacy.

Chapter 12 Developing Your Trading Plan

Having a strong trading plan is an important part of successfully trading on the Forex market. Even the experts develop one, so it is important that as a beginner, you do too. In this chapter, you are going to learn about why you need a roadmap and how you can develop one.

What Is a Trading Plan?

Developing a trading plan allows you to define a goal and create a system for you to work towards that goal through your trades. Due to the volatility of the market, you cannot create a finite blueprint for your trading plan. However, you can create a general strategy and goals for you to work with. There are certain rules and elements to consider when you are developing your plan to ensure that you have one that is strong and will serve you for the best.

Who Needs One?

It is important that anyone who is doing trading on the Forex market, or anywhere else for that matter, to have a strong trading plan. This allows them the opportunity to reap in all of the benefits of having a trading plan from risk management to learning discipline in your trades. Even experts develop plans before entering the Forex market, so it is imperative that as a beginner, you also develop a plan.

Why Do You Need a Trading Plan?

There are a number of benefits to having a trading plan when you are getting involved in the Forex market. For one, it is great for you to minimize your risk due to your ability to have a plan for what you will do in certain scenarios. You can also use it to establish your exit strategies beforehand so that you know when you are going to exit if necessary. Having a plan also allows you to stay focused on your goal and make large strides towards that goal, so you can stay on par for your goals with your trading decisions. Another reason why having a plan is important is because it allows you to ensure that you are constantly evaluating your trades to ensure that your money is working well for you and that you are making strong decisions. If you find that your trades aren't having high enough yields or are too risky, you can reevaluate your plan and fix your strategy for a better outcome.

General Planning Rules

There are a few plans when you are preparing to trade on the market. There are no blueprints, though there are some considerations you need to think about when you are developing the plan. The following four "rules" are important when you are in the process of creating your trading plan, to ensure that you have the best results.

- Write down your goals all the time. If you make any changes, write that down as well. You will want to write down virtually every single part of your plan. This way, you can ensure that your thoughts are organized and your plan is solid. It also helps you stay focused on your goals and work towards them with every move you make.

- Make sure that in addition to writing out your plans, you record your progress as well. This allows you to see how your plan has worked, and to learn from previous trades that you have made as well so that you can continue to learn and make better decisions. This process will give you a better opportunity to improve your trading strategies and ensure that you recall which markets you have been exposed to.

- Aside from writing everything down, you must control your finances. It is important that you manage your money properly in order to ensure that you are staying on top of everything to prevent yourself from investing too much into the market. You want to make sure that you are managing your risk and exposure and staying on top of how much you are making and losing in the grand scheme of things.

The best way to keep track of everything is to have a trading journal that allows you to keep track of your plan and all of the moves you make. It also allows you to keep track of your finances to ensure that you are making wise decisions and not investing too much or losing too much in certain moves.

Creating Your Plan

Before you create a plan, you need to ask yourself some questions. You should write these questions down in your trading journal to ensure that you are focused on what your goal is and that your plan aligns with the answers you have for the following questions.

- Why do you want to trade with Forex?
- What is your opinion on risk?
- What is the amount of time you're willing to invest in trades?
- How much do you know about trading already?

Identifying the answers to these questions is the best way to discover what your goals are with trading and how you position yourself in the market on trades that you will make. You need to answer these questions before you start creating your plan, as they are the basis for the plans that you make.

Once you answer those four primary questions, there are more you will want to consider. The answer to these will be exactly what you need to know in order to create your specific plan and move forward with it. Your answers don't need to be deep and thoughtful, but they do need to be answered clearly.

- Where are you right now, financially? Have you had any involvement in the market yet? If so, what is your involvement?

- At this time, what type of trader are you? What are your thoughts on trading and risk?

- Based on your level of knowledge right now, how confident do you feel in trading?

- What is the amount of capital you have to start your trading with?

- What are your financial goals with your trading?

- How long do you want to be trading for in order to reach that goal?

What is the success going to look like?

Answering these questions gives you a firm guideline of where you want to go and what you want to do with your trading. If you go in saying "I want to make a lot of money" but never define what "a lot" is, you are not going to be able to identify when you get there. You will also not know how to identify if you have been losing too much money. The market is something that you enter for specific purposes, as that is what will assist you in making the money you desire. You don't necessarily need to have a purpose such as retirement or education funds, but having a goal of what you want and a timeframe of when you want to achieve it will significantly assist you in mastering it and making as much as you desire.

Conclusion

By now you should already have a good foundation of what it the FX market is about, as well as how you can be a successful trader. The forex market is a challenging place. It does not care about you and how you feel. To make a profit, you also have to make the right decisions every time. The good news is that it is possible to turn the forex market into a goldmine. What you need to do now is to continue to learn as much as you can about forex and start developing your strategy. If this is your first time to trade, then it is strongly advised that you begin with a demo account, so that you can test the water without risking anything. If you think and feel that trading foreign currencies is the one for you, then you can make a deposit and start trading with real money at any time.

Many people are making lots of income, even a full-time income, trading currencies in the comfort of their home. If you ever dream of doing the same, then know that it is doable. The FX market is a big market that generates trillions of dollars every trading day. However, this kind of opportunity does not turn into a goldmine unless you dedicate enough time for regular practice and hard work.

You can also expect to make some mistakes from time to time. Do not worry; committing mistakes is a normal part of being an FX trader. The important thing is that you learn from every mistake that you make. Every mistake presents an opportunity to make you a better trader.

How about financial freedom? Yes, the forex market can be your place for financial freedom. Many people from around the globe make lots of money by trading foreign currencies. Although this is not a quick get-rich scheme, it is possible to be rich by being an FX trader. Although there is no guarantee of success, the more efforts, and study that you put into every trade, the closer you get to achieving financial freedom.

The forex market is a complex world, and everyone is trying to look for the goose that lays the golden egg. In this case, we are talking about that one trade that will simply propel someone to new heights.

People imagine that getting into the forex market is easy, that pretty soon they will be diving into cash the way Scrooge McDuck takes a joyful dive in his pile of gold coins.

That rarely happens. But the prospect of making some incredible profits still exists, provided you are ready to navigate the complexities of the forex market.

In fact, here is something you should know.

This is a real market. It is the largest financial market in the world, and you have to treat it as such. You can trade this market part-time, or you can do it every day. In fact, you can make it your business—the business of trading.

People have actually quit their day jobs to get into the world of forex trading. However, that is something that you should not even consider if you are starting out. Do not make rash decisions in the hope that you are going to master the markets and strike rich in no time. Those are wonderful ambitions but are not backed by experience.

You see, trading can be learned, of course, but the experience can't be transmitted.

It has to be constructed by every individual through a personal effort of understanding and hard work.

Another thing that is important to understand is that you will never ever stop learning. Markets are changing every day, and the forex is a living organism that evolves in the same way as all its traders. Always remember that although it seems to be an unknown entity, at the end of the day, the market is merely made up of investors, large and small, from all corners of the world, each with his or her own emotions, psychology, and predictable behaviors and reactions.

Do you ever walk up to a doctor and ask him or her if there is a shortcut to reaching where he or she has reached? Would you do that to an engineer or a renowned sportsperson? These people have developed their skills over time. They have honed their abilities as much as possible before they could use them fluently.

It is the same with the forex market. You might need to put in your efforts to learn the tricks of the trade (no pun intended).

Learn to move on after losses. Don't dwell on missed trades or missed pips after you decide to close. There will be hundreds of opportunities in the future. Follow your plan, and follow your system. Practice every day, and experience will come with time, patience, and discipline. Don't look outside for what's already inside. Leave your ego behind; be humble and smart. You can't decide where the market will go, so learn to see where it wants to lead you, not the other way around. Exit bad trades, and hold on to good trades. Set yourself a goal and stop trading when you have reached it.

www.ingramcontent.com/pod-product-compliance
Lightning Source LLC
Chambersburg PA
CBHW071400210526
45465CB00001B/181